The Thinking Teacher's Toolkit

Also available from Continuum

Teaching Critical Thinking Skills – Mal Leicester
Teaching Thinking, 3rd edition – Robert Fisher
Teaching Thinking Skills – Stephen Johnson, Harvey Siegel and Christopher Winch
100+ Ideas for Teaching Thinking Skills – Steve Bowkett

The Thinking Teacher's Toolkit

Critical Thinking, Thinking Skills
and Global Perspectives

Ruth Matthews and Jo Lally

continuum

Continuum International Publishing Group

The Tower Building   80 Maiden Lane Suite 704
11 York Road   New York NY 10038
London
SE1 7NX

www.continuumbooks.com

British Library Cataloguing-in-Publication Data
A catalogue record for this book is available from the British Library.

ISBN: 978-1-4411-2571-2 (paperback)

Library of Congress Cataloging-in-Publication Data
A catalog record for this book is available from the Library of Congress.

Typeset by Free Range Book Design & Production Ltd
Printed and bound in Great Britain by the MPG Books Group

A companion website to accompany this book is available online at:
http://education.matthewslally.continuumbooks.com.

Please visit the link and register with us to receive your password and to access these downloadable resources.

If you experience any problems accessing the resources, please contact Continuum at: info@continuumbooks.com.

Contents

Key to Icons

 Online

 Log book

 Discussion

 Comment

 Activity

Introduction

In the course of our work with hundreds of teachers and examiners involved in the delivery and assessment of thinking skills, we have identified the need for a practical guide. This book has been designed to provide a toolkit for teachers who teach thinking skills, reasoning and critical thinking to 14–19 age groups. If you've just discovered you're now your school's thinking skills specialist, this book will answer your basic questions and help you to build on your existing expertise. If you have greater experience of this curriculum area, it will help to enhance your professional skills.

This book starts from the presumption that, even if you have never knowingly taught thinking skills before, you already possess relevant expertise, but may not be fully aware of how best to apply it. The toolkit approach means possibilities – the tools – are presented, from which you can select the tool for a given task. The sections do not need to be read in sequence: they stand alone so that you can dip in as you need.

Everything you require to become a thinking teacher is packed into the toolkit, including guidance on setting up a thinking skills course from scratch, strategies for delivering thinking and reasoning skills as a discrete subject, approaches to integrating thinking skills within other subjects, ideas for selecting and designing resources, and advice on preparing students for external assessment. In addition, there are online resources to accompany this book, including material for student activities, CPD activities and FAQs.

At the time of writing, the authors had between them over twenty years' experience of working for awarding bodies operating within the UK and internationally. They have unique thinking skills subject knowledge and understanding of course design, together with unparalleled experience of assessment methodologies and insight into the difficulties teachers face in teaching thinking skills and critical thinking.

This book is primarily for the classroom teacher who is delivering – and possibly also planning – courses and qualifications that contain a significant element of thinking and reasoning skills (including the CIE Global Perspectives syllabuses and the Diploma qualifications) within the 14–19 curriculum. It will also be of interest to anyone who wishes to improve their understanding of strategies for planning and teaching thinking skills, including practising teachers, teacher trainers, trainee teachers, curriculum managers, 11–19 teachers and higher education lecturers in a range of disciplines.

How Does this Book Help?

The book's focus is the design and implementation of activities which enhance students' thinking and engage their interest and enthusiasm. It:

- contains strategies for course and lesson planning;
- includes ideas for activities, tips and tricks for teaching, and ways in which the subject can be taught effectively in a reduced timetable slot;
- provides guidance on how to select and use an appropriate examination syllabus;
- considers how students' achievement in examinations can be maximised, whilst ensuring that students are enthusiastic, motivated, and fully aware of the purpose of developing these skills;
- draws on relevant research findings, to provide a starting point for further continuing professional development.

Part 1 sets out tools for teaching. The teacher who is a complete novice will find the skills outlined in Chapter 1, together with lesson plans and suggestions for their first ever lesson on thinking skills. If you are an experienced teacher you could skip straight to Chapter 2 (see page 28), but you may still find the ideas in Chapter 1 interesting and useful. Chapter 2 considers approaches to teaching thinking and reasoning skills and discusses how to find a balance between practising skills explicitly in order to improve them and practising skills embedded in a meaningful context. Chapter 3 discusses the issues involved in planning a course that includes a significant element of thinking and reasoning skills, including applying approaches from Chapter 2 in the context of real schools and colleges. Chapter 4 considers lesson planning, lesson ideas and practical approaches. It explains how a variety of approaches can be adapted to work in real situations. Chapter 5 provides ideas for developing your own original resources, selecting and adapting source material. It considers what makes resources or a passage work as a class exercise.

Part 2 sets out tools for enhancing achievement. Chapter 6 provides supporting, background information for the teacher who wishes to raise the profile of thinking skills within their institution. The benefits of teaching thinking skills are outlined. There is a brief history of the development of thinking skills approaches and an explanation of what thinking skills are and what they are not. The chapter introduces the central theoretical approaches that underpin successful teaching strategies. Thinking skills both support the wider curriculum and offer countless opportunities for curriculum enrichment. Chapter 7 considers the advantages and disadvantages of different approaches: critical thinking as a discrete subject; the infusion approach where critical thinking is taught across the curriculum; and integrating critical thinking in a specific subject. There are ideas for integrating critical thinking within subject teaching, with sample activities for vocational subjects, English literature and religious studies.

Part 3 sets out tools for assessment. Education is increasingly assessment-driven, and tests of thinking skills and critical thinking have burgeoned in the last 20 years. Chapter 8 explains the main public examinations that students encounter and gives guidance on preparing students for the particular demands of these assessments. It gives pointers towards ways of enhancing students' performance in thinking skills or critical thinking examinations. Chapter 9 explains what you should expect from an examination board and discusses possible courses of action if students' results do not meet expectations.

Part 4 is available online at http://education.matthewslally. continuumbooks.com and sets out tools for developing your professional expertise. It provides a quick reference where answers can be found to frequently asked questions about setting up new courses and teaching thinking skills and critical thinking. It includes suggestions for wider reading in the field of thinking skills and information on popular and useful resources. These will save you the time and tedium of searching for good resources.

The authors are writing from the standpoint of considerable experience of teaching and assessing thinking skills, but – as critical thinkers writing for critical thinkers – they do not claim that all the ideas in this book will work in every classroom situation. The best tool for any given lesson needs to be picked out of the toolkit, and then used correctly.

Key Definitions

Since John Dewey developed the concept of reflective thinking around a hundred years ago, education researchers and teachers have been attempting to incorporate thinking skills approaches into teaching. Nonetheless, many teachers have – at best – a hazy concept of what 'thinking skills', 'reasoning skills' and 'critical thinking' mean, what they have in common, and how they differ. These terms are used imprecisely and interchangeably by many commentators. Different interpretations will be explored further in Part 2, but in this book the meanings given below are used.

Thinking Skills are the skills needed to think analytically, logically and creatively to form reasoned judgements and solve problems. As specified by the National Curriculum framework for England, the thinking skills are 'information processing, reasoning, enquiry, creative thinking and evaluation' (DfES, 2002).

Reasoning is the act or process of drawing inferences and conclusions from information, facts, evidence, etc. *Reasoning skills* involve clarifying meaning, explaining, analysing, opinion forming, decision making, interpreting and giving reasons for conclusions.

Critical thinking is reasonable, reflective thinking that is focused on deciding what to believe or do. It has become established as an academic discipline that involves examining beliefs, knowledge and information in the light of supporting evidence and any conclusions that can be drawn. Some critical thinking practitioners (and examination syllabuses) focus on analysis and evaluation of *argument*, which is intended to be persuasive by presenting one or more reasons to support a conclusion. Other commentators take a wider view: 'Critical Thinking is reasonable, reflective thinking that is focused on deciding what to believe or do' (Ennis, October 2000, at www.criticalthinking.net).

Problem solving demands the skills of reasoning and creative thinking: reasoning to define and analyse the problem, creative thinking to generate possible solutions, and reasoning again to select the preferred solution. Assessments in problem solving usually test understanding of information, data handling, modelling, logic and reasoning, rather than the creative generation of solutions.

Global Perspectives are qualifications designed to embed thinking and reasoning skills in issues of global importance. Students are expected to reflect on and reason about issues in a global context, and to develop the ability to reflect on their own thinking. Global Perspectives is examined by Cambridge International Examinations as an International GCSE and within the Cambridge Pre-U Diploma (as part of Global Perspectives and Independent Research Report). Both qualifications place emphasis on students developing the skills needed to cope with increasing globalisation and the multiplicity of competing ideas, arguments and information available via the internet, and to deal with competing perspectives and ideas sensitively.

Part 1

Tools for Teaching

Introduction to Part 1

This is a toolkit to enable you to build your own resources and library of teaching strategies, not a flat-pack construct which will fall apart the first time it is tested.

Who is a Thinking Teacher?

The thinking teacher might teach a subject with a significant element of thinking and reasoning skills tested explicitly. Equally, the thinking teacher might encourage students to develop the ability to think and reason critically in the context of a more traditional subject. Although this book is aimed predominantly at the former, the latter will also find much that is useful, because it is generally good practice to teach thinking skills in context and to keep a firm eye on how to apply and embed explicitly taught thinking skills to real life and academic contexts. Explicit teaching and practising of skills is often necessary, but is rarely effective unless some thought is given to their application and use.

The Courses

Rather than referring to specific courses, the practical guidance contained in the first five chapters will refer to Level 2 and Level 3 courses. Level 2 courses include, but are not limited to, OCR Thinking and Reasoning Skills and CIE IGCSE Global Perspectives. Level 3 courses include, but are not limited to, AQA and OCR A Levels in Critical Thinking, CIE A Level Thinking Skills and CIE Pre-U Global Perspectives. Teachers of other courses not mentioned here may also find much that is useful. In Chapter 6 there is a thorough consideration of many of the thinking and reasoning skills courses available worldwide.

Health Warning!

This book aims to help teachers develop successful strategies for teaching thinking and reasoning skills. It is not a substitute for the specification or syllabus, question papers, mark schemes and examiners' reports of the qualification you are working with. It is intended to complement and supplement textbooks and teacher resources aimed at particular qualifications.

Because of the very nature of thinking and reasoning skills, much of the first five chapters, which focus on practical teaching and learning, will consist of suggestions, questions and discussions. There are a number of qualifications that include a significant element of thinking and reasoning skills, and a useful suggestion for GCE Critical Thinking AS may be less useful for IGCSE Global Perspectives, or an idea which works for teachers of the CHEER Skills Development Programme may need considerable adaptation to work for a teacher of GCE A Level Thinking Skills or Pre-U Global Perspectives and Independent Research Report. On the other hand, these qualifications have a core of common aims, so many of the ideas in this book can be used for several qualifications with some adaptation. Ultimately, it will be up to the thinking teacher to choose solutions and find strategies which suit them, their students and the qualifications they are working on.

Log Book

While you are reading this book you may find it useful to record any thoughts provoked by the teaching and planning discussions. You may also wish to have a dedicated space for working through some of the activities, which you can refer to later. One way of doing this is to use a log book, which can also act as a professional journal, allowing you to reflect on your own practice and the response of students to activities you try. This may very often be brief: 'Tried new activity – noisy – much thinking. How to formalise?' However, it can also be a space for working through difficulties, and when things don't work it can help you to realise why, inspiring strategies for improvement.

1   The Starting Point

The purpose of this chapter is to provide a starting point, or way into teaching thinking and reasoning skills, for those who are new to it. However, more experienced practitioners will also gain ideas to inform their teaching and planning. As you work through this chapter, you may find it useful to refer back to definitions of thinking and reasoning skills given in the introduction (see page 4).

The First Lesson

The first lesson of any new subject can be nerve-racking. This is especially the case for thinking teachers, many of whom have been informed with little notice that they are the school's new specialist. There is also no subject matter and few resources to fall back on, just a collection of skills that you think you ought to have, but aren't quite sure that you actually do.

It is natural to feel apprehensive without the security of degree-level knowledge and tried and tested notes and lesson plans. Starting to teach thinking and reasoning skills is undoubtedly a challenge, but it is also one of the most liberating experiences in teaching, and one of the most empowering for your students. Your subject matter can be whatever you want it to be, so long as it provokes your students to think. And your skills can be polished up and tweaked to suit the qualification you are working with.

We will first look at two ideas for lessons, and then consider what the thinking skills are, what they're for, and how you can use those you already have.

Lesson Idea One: decision making

The following dialogue can be used as a starting point to link rather abstract thinking and reasoning skills to real life. It can readily be extended to develop more academic applications of thinking and reasoning skills. It can be used for either Level 2 or Level 3 courses – but if you are teaching a Level 3 course it is as well to check which students have already taken a Level 2 course involving thinking and reasoning skills, to make sure you avoid repeating a task they have already done.

Donna: *I've decided I'm going to leave school because it's really boring and I want to get married to Mark. I'm not learning anything useful, and I think I'd be better off getting a job.*

Mum: *But you're only 16!*

Donna: *And?*

Mum: *And that's too young. You'll wreck your life. You'll be tied to someone you hate and have no prospects of your own.*

Dad: *I read somewhere that 33 per cent of people who leave school at 16 are unemployed. That's not what we want for you Donna. We want you to have a good life.*

Donna: *Dad, I know you want what's best, but I'm grown up now. I know what's best for me and it's not school. Who cares what happened in 1831?*

Dad: *Donna, love, it's not about what happened in 1831, it's about the future. Education can give you options for the future. If you've got qualifications you can do all sorts of different jobs, and people take you more seriously. So you really ought to get your qualifications.*

Donna: *Well, my friend Karen's friend's mum got married at 17, and she's still happy, and she's got three children and she enjoys working in the supermarket. She says leaving school early and having children was the best thing she could have done.*

Mum: *No way, Donna. While we're paying for you, you'll stay in education.*

Donna: *That's the point, Mum. Me and Mark will be paying for ourselves and making our own decisions.*

Mum: *Actually, you won't. You need our permission to get married before you're 18.*

The next section includes a variety of different activities that could be used with this dialogue as a starting point. The amount of time you have, and level of course you are teaching, will affect how deep you take the discussion in each section, and even whether this is a single lesson or a series of two or three. In the first, it might be useful to ensure a broad coverage of the various skills, to act as an introduction.

Activities

General discussion

- What do you think Donna should do? Why?
- Would you make the same choices as Donna? Why (not)?
- What are the differences between you and Donna? How do these differences affect your choice?
- Is there a 'right' answer in this situation?
- How can we ever know what to do? / How do we make important decisions?
- What sort of things can help us to know what is best / what to do?
- How can we ever know what is true?
- Can we ever know anything at all?

Comment

This general discussion allows students to explore their own personal perspectives and consider how they are grounded. Students might start to think about the difference between justifying what they already think and adapting their view in the light of questioning the evidence. You may like to introduce the well-known quotation by Keynes: 'When the facts change, I change my mind. What do you do, sir?' Push students to think beyond the obvious, and expect them always to justify what they think. Perhaps ask them to consider the different roles that emotions and reason have in decision making. Is it ever right to make a decision which your head tells you is wrong but your instinct tells you is right? Expect more of Level 3 students than Level 2.

How do you know that?

Each question is followed by suggestions for discussion. These are not the 'answers' – it is most important that students think for themselves and start to reason and support their ideas.

Dad says, 'I read somewhere that 33 per cent of people who leave school at 16 are unemployed.' How reliable is this? Why? (If you think it is unreliable, does that make it definitely wrong?)

Dad's statistic is a bit dubious. 'I read somewhere' is rather vague, so we don't know whether this is a reputable source which checks its facts or a sensationalising one which purposely misconstrues statistics for effect. Dad suggests he might have misremembered. We are also uncertain about the context – is this short- or long-term unemployment? However, none of this means that the statistic is definitely wrong, just that we need to be a bit wary.

Does this mean that Donna will definitely be unemployed if she leaves school at 16?

Even if the statistic is accurate, it doesn't mean that Donna will definitely be unemployed. If she is talking of leaving school only after she has found a job, then the statistic is irrelevant. If she already has Level 2 qualifications, good teamwork and people skills and is prepared to work hard, she will have a better chance at a job than someone with no qualifications and poor people skills.

Do you think Donna's friend Karen's friend's mum is a good example? Why? Does *her* happiness affect Donna's likelihood of being happy?

Donna's friend Karen's friend's mum does show that it is possible for someone who marries early to be happy, if she is being truthful and not just justifying her decision or making the best of her situation. We need to be careful about this kind of hearsay evidence, because it might have become twisted or exaggerated as it was passed from one person to another. We also need to be aware that Donna's friend Karen's friend's mum may not be typical. We would need a lot more evidence about the situation before we made a judgement. Even if she is happy after marrying young, this doesn't mean that Donna will be happy; Donna's happiness will depend on her own personality, choices and situation.

Do you think Donna's parents are good people to advise her? Why (not)?

Donna's parents might be good people to advise Donna. This depends on many factors. What sort of people are they? How well do they get on with Donna? Do they want to guide Donna or live her life for her? Does Donna respect their views? Do they make good decisions in their own lives? Donna's parents do have more life experience than her. Parents are important figures in our lives; it is natural to honour and even believe them, but also to rebel against them. So whether they are good people to advise Donna depends also on whether she honours or is rebelling against them.

Who else should Donna ask for advice?

Some people that Donna might ask are: her friends, a religious adviser, Mark, a careers adviser, her grandparents, a financial adviser. Sources that she might consider investigating include job adverts, careers websites, and even social networking sites such as mumsnet, where she might get more advice from people who have made choices like hers. These lists could be very much longer.

What sort of information should Donna look for / what else does Donna need to know to inform her decision?

She should be looking for personal experience, financial advice and careers advice to help her make the best choices.

What would affect the reliability of the advice given to Donna by the people/sources you have suggested?

Encourage students to think as deeply as they can and consider who could provide what sort of advice, and how reliable it would be.

How much does it matter if a source of information isn't 100 per cent reliable?

It is important to consider how much it matters if a source of information isn't 100 per cent reliable. It is unlikely that any source is 100 per cent reliable, as this is a very high standard So it would be rash to completely discard *fairly* reliable evidence. The information from a fairly reliable source can be considered alongside other sources, and the evidence weighed.

Comment
The above questions focus on the reliability and use of evidence, and the strength of conclusions that can be drawn. They are important in understanding how we do, and how we should, build up our ideas about issues, other people and the world – that is, our beliefs and knowledge.

continued

At this stage, it is probably best to keep the discussion general, nudging it so that students arrive for themselves at the idea that some sources of evidence, and some forms of 'knowledge', are better than others, and begin to articulate why. Later in the course you can start to formalise this understanding. At the end of this first lesson you could tell students that they will learn a lot more about these forms of thinking and their uses.

Types of reasoning

Introduce the following types of reasoning (either by displaying the online version, or by asking students to match key terms and definitions):

- *Persuading*: trying to get someone else to agree with your view. This may be done with reasons and / or through emotions.
- *Arguing*: giving reasons to support a view, in order to persuade others to accept the view.
- *Explaining*: saying how or why something is the way it is.
- *Ranting*: speaking vehemently or at length, trying to persuade, often in an emotive rather than reasoned way.
- *Giving opinion*: saying what you believe about something.
- *Giving evidence*: giving facts and figures, personal anecdotes, information from a variety of sources.
- *Making predictions*: saying what you think will happen.

Note that these categories can overlap. Arguing is one form of rational persuasion. It can often include giving opinions and facts, making predictions. Ranting can include weak argument.

At this point you may wish to reinforce the distinction between arguing which gives reasons to support a conclusion and arguing which becomes unpleasantly personal in the everyday quarrelling sense of argument. It would also be useful to ask students to put together some rules for class discussions and arguments. These might include, 'Listen to others', and 'Don't be personal or abusive'.

Ask students to reread the dialogue and see if they can find:

1. An explanation:
   Donna: *I've decided I'm going to leave school because it's really boring and I want to get married to Mark.* (Donna here is telling her parents why she has taken a decision.)

2. An argument:

   Dad: *Education can give you options for the future. If you've got qualifications you can do all sorts of different jobs, and people take you more seriously. So you really ought to get your qualifications.* (Dad is trying to persuade Donna to get her qualifications by giving her reasons why.)

3. A prediction:

   Mum: *You'll wreck your life / You'll be tied to someone you hate and have no prospects of your own.* (Mum is making dire predictions about the awful consequences that will come of leaving school early to get married. Note that not every sentence in the future tense or about the future is a prediction. When Donna says she's going to leave school, she is expressing an intention, and when Mum says, 'you'll stay in education', she is giving an order.)

4. An attempt to persuade with emotions and opinions.

   Mum: *And that's too young. You'll wreck your life. You'll be tied to someone you hate and have no prospects of your own.* (None of Mum's claims here give us any reason to believe any of the others, so she is not arguing or explaining. She is, however, trying to persuade Donna through an emotional portrait of what her life might be like.)

5. Someone giving evidence.

   Dad: *I read somewhere that 33 per cent of people who leave school at 16 are unemployed.*

Comment

The above activity introduces some of the different kinds of reasoning that are used in daily life, the media and academic study. Ask students to think of areas in which different kinds of reasoning are used. Scientific reasoning, for example, makes great use of explanation. Begin to discuss the rational strength of different kinds of reasoning, questioning which of these forms of reasoning gives us better grounds for believing/thinking we know something? For example, a scientific explanation backed by experimental evidence, or a logical argument with good reasons to support a conclusion, is more likely to give us reasonably secure knowledge than a rant or 'evidence' arriving by a hearsay route. Tell students that they will learn more about these forms of reasoning and their uses during the course.

Assessing the impact of additional information
Give students the additional information below.

> **Elisha, Donna's friend:** *Donna, don't be stupid. If you love each other, you can wait a couple of years before you get married. Out of your whole life, a couple of years isn't much. Otherwise you'll end up like my mum. She's got no qualifications, and just looks after me and Dad. She's bored and frustrated and doesn't believe she can do anything about it. She can't buy herself anything without checking with Dad, because it's all his money. She's stuck in a life she doesn't like. Really, you don't want to be like her. Get engaged now if you want to, but you'd be mad to leave school and get married.*
>
> **Careers Adviser:** *Well, Donna, there are some options that might suit you. You're good with numbers and with people, so you might enjoy working in a bank. Look at this scheme from the National Bank. They give you experience in four different areas of the bank over two years, and then you can specialise. They will support you to get professional qualifications in the area you choose. Or you could join this chain of department stores as a trainee. They give you the choice between specialising in one area, or working towards management. This particular chain has an excellent reputation for dealing with parents with young children. They'll let you work flexible hours, and also support you through training programmes at your own pace. You really should think about the sort of job that gives you future options, Donna. You're intelligent and capable of having a really satisfying career. Right now you're in love, and you want to get married and have children. That's fine. But it's important to keep living your own life too.*

Do these extra sources of information alter your view about what Donna should do? How? Why?

Discuss with students the extent to which each of these passages affects their view of the situation. For example, does the additional information about possible jobs with training opportunities and career structures make Donna's possible future as a married school leaver seem less bleak and therefore less inadvisable? Does Elisha's advice to get engaged rather than married offer a useful alternative perspective? Does either person offer an argument? How strong is Elisha's example of her own mother?

Presenting reasoning

Ask students to do one or more of the following:

- Prepare and perform a dialogue in which one student persuades Donna as emotionally as possible to stay at school.
- Answer the following question: 'Should Donna stay at school or get a job?' Give reasons to support your view.
- Compare the kinds of reasoning used in each task, and consider which might give Donna a stronger basis for making a decision.
- Answer the following question: 'To what extent can Donna *know* she is making the right decision?'
- Consider economic, moral and social perspectives on the issue of post-16 education and come to a reasoned view whether it should be compulsory for young people to stay in education until they are 18.
- Answer the following questions: 'In the UK 16- to 17-year-olds need permission from their parents to get married. Do you think this is reasonable? How does this law compare with laws in other countries?' Students might again consider the different sorts of reasoning used to answer these questions.

Further activities

The starter lessons we have just discussed could easily lead into one or more of the following activities:

- Work on the reliability and use of evidence in argument (e.g. Critical Thinking).
- Consideration of different standards of knowledge and certainty (e.g. Knowledge and Inquiry).
- A short research project on families (perhaps starting with the question, 'Is marriage equally important around the world?'), leading to a presentation. (e.g. IGCSE Global Perspectives).
- A consideration of the economic role of women and its relationship to quality of life, critically considering the evidence base for different perspectives on this issue, leading to an essay (e.g. Pre-U Global Perspectives).

Discussion: talking through the course outline and aims

Neither Lesson Idea One (above) nor Lesson Idea Two (below) includes a detailed look at the course outline. Students do need to gain an idea of what their course involves and what they should be able to do by the end of it. However, because thinking and reasoning differs in many ways from traditional subjects, it is worth discussing at what point, in what detail, and in what way students can come by this understanding. Let's consider and discuss a number of options:

Option A

Lesson One: Talk students through the syllabus and tell them about exam requirements.
Lesson Two: Start teaching proper, perhaps with one of the lesson ideas introduced here.

Advantages of Option A

- This is a clear and logical progression.
- This option is easy to organise and manage.
- Students may expect to be told about the course at the beginning.

Disadvantages of Option A

- Students may have to sit through several similar introductions to their courses, Students may have insufficient understanding of the subject to follow an outline of the syllabus. It may well be meaningful to students in a traditional subject to say, 'We are going to study Stalin's power politics', or 'The first part of the course is twentieth-century American poetry.' However, in a newer subject, where you are introducing thinking and reasoning skills, students may simply not know what you mean when you say, 'First, we are going to study the reliability of evidence, then we will look at the structure of reasoning.' Such language may perplex students, and possibly drive them away.

Option B

Lesson One: Lesson Idea One or Two used as an introduction.
Lesson Two: Talk students through the syllabus briefly and tell them about exam requirements. Begin teaching proper, perhaps building on Lesson Idea One or Two.

Advantages of Option B

- Students have the opportunity to put some skills into practice, so they have more understanding of what you mean when you say, 'We are going to start by considering the reliability of evidence.'
- Students generally enjoy interactive lessons, so they should come out of Lesson One buzzing with enthusiasm.
- This option is also easy to manage.

Disadvantages of Option B

- This option is not quite as logical as Option A – it feels messier.
- It may feel as if you are interrupting teaching to talk about syllabus and exam requirements.
- You may lose momentum.

Option C

Start with an introductory cycle of three or four lessons, touching on many of the required skills, possibly using one or both of the lesson ideas introduced here. At the beginning of the cycle, tell students very briefly that they are going to start practising thinking and reasoning skills in the context of making decisions and/or forming judgements.

As each skill is touched on, explain that the course will cover it in more depth. At the end of the introductory cycle of lessons, talk briefly through the exam structure, telling students which skills are included in each part of the assessment. It might be useful to include a formative assessment at this point, to help students decide whether the course is right for them.

Advantages of Option C

- Gives students the opportunity to gain a very good idea of what the course will be like by experiencing the different skills in a practical context.
- Is likely to be engaging and interesting.
- Should help students to see the point of the different thinking and reasoning skills as a means to an end.
- Works with the nature of learning as a spiral in which concepts are revisited.
- Introductory issues such as library/resource centre use can be integrated and related to the skills – assessing the reliability of evidence is clearly relevant to the selection of material when using the library or internet, for example.

Disadvantages of Option C

- Is by far the hardest option to plan and manage.
- If not tightly managed, can seem disorganised.
- Might not appeal to teachers or students who like to take one thing at a time.

We have a personal preference for Option C, but you shouldn't necessarily accept it. What is your preference? What will work best for you and your students? If you prefer a clear, logical, linear progression, how can you deal with the disadvantages of Option A? Can you, perhaps, reduce the detail of the introduction?

Lesson Idea Two: forming judgements

This second lesson idea concentrates on the idea of forming judgements based on report, evidence and argument. It is perhaps more suited to Level 3 students, but it would certainly be possible to use it with able Level 2 students.

Because they were worth it? Research finds Neanderthals enjoyed makeup

For decades, our low-browed Neanderthal cousins have been portrayed as dim savages whose idea of seduction was a whispered 'ug' and a blow to the cranium.

But analysis of pierced, hand-coloured shells and lumps of pigment from two caves in south-east Spain suggests the cave-people who stomped around Europe 50,000 years ago were far more intelligent – and cosmetically minded – than previously thought.

In 1985, archaeologists excavating the Cueva de los Aviones in Murcia found cockle shells perforated as if to be hung on a necklace and an oyster shell containing mineral pigments, hinting that the cave's Neanderthal residents had developed a taste for self-adornment and makeup.

Twenty-three years later, an expedition led by João Zilhão, professor of Palaeolithic archaeology at the University of Bristol, turned up a pierced, orange-coloured scallop shell bearing traces of red and yellow pigment at another Murcian cave, Cueva Antón.

Despite its significance, however, the latter find was nearly overlooked.

'The shell was found by an undergraduate student at Bristol on the first or second day of the dig,' said Zilhão. 'When he showed it to me I told him it was probably a fossil from the cave wall. Note it and bag it, I said, we'll look at it later. We forgot about it till later and then, when we were cleaning it, I realised that it was a shell, not a fossil.'

It was then, said the professor, that it occurred to him the shell might corroborate the finds at Cueva de los Aviones, and prove that Neanderthals were more sophisticated than they had been given credit for.

Analysis of the reddish residues from the oyster shell from Cueva de los Aviones had found a pigment made up of minerals including lepidocrocite, haematite, pyrite, and charcoal. The orange scallop shell found in Cueva Antón, meanwhile, had been coloured with red haematite and yellow goethite and was probably part of a necklace.

The small quantity of pigment recovered in the oyster shell also led the archaeologists to speculate that it had been made for use on the body. According to Zilhão, the effect of the darkly sparkling preparation would not have been too different from today's coruscating skin powders.

'The idea that came to our minds was that it was some kind of glitter or makeup like the shimmery stuff that people were wearing a few years ago,' he said.

continued

continued

'Its preparation makes no sense unless it was used as a body cosmetic. We can't prove it but it makes sense.'

As well as yielding evidence of mining, transportation and the ability to work to a complex recipe, said Zilhão, the existence of the cosmetics also provides an insight into Neanderthal psychology. 'They are clearly used as something to convey ideas and to decorate the face and body. It shows a symbolic dimension in behaviour and thinking that cannot be denied – especially when found in connection with the perforated and decorated shells.'

What's more, said the professor, the oyster shell, which was also held in high esteem by cultures in pre-Columbian America, was also found near a quantity of yellow natrojarosite, a mineral pigment whose cosmetic properties made it a favourite of the ancient Egyptians.

Radiocarbon dating of the samples was carried out by the University of Oxford's radiocarbon accelerator unit. Their tests established that the shells and charcoal found in the two caves could be traced back to around 50,000 years ago – around 10 millennia before the first appearance in Europe of early modern man. All of which, reckons Zilhão, shows that Neanderthals were doing many of the same things as their early modern human counterparts in Africa.

'Whether that means that the Neanderthals were as smart as early modern humans or that early modern humans were as stupid as Neanderthals depends on how you look at the past,' he said. 'My view is that there's absolutely no scientific justification to consider Neanderthals as the brutish halfwits they have been portrayed as in popular culture – which has also, to a certain extent, influenced scientific thinking.'

It was high time, he added, to banish our caveman prejudices. 'Even if they were a bit different in behaviour and cognition, they were as human as their contemporaries, who we call our ancestors.'

The findings are published in the journal *Proceedings of the National Academy of Sciences*. (See www.guardian.co.uk/science/2010/jan/11/caveman-neanderthal-makeup-spain.)

Activities

As with Lesson Idea One, you may need to pick and choose which of the following questions to discuss in more detail, depending on the time available to you, the level of your students, and which qualification you are working towards.

General discussion

- What do you know about Neanderthals?
- How do you know? How reliable is this knowledge?
- What sort of problems are there in forming judgements about conditions in the world 50,000 years ago?

Comment

Encourage students to think along the lines of finding, interpreting, using evidence, making inferences from the evidence, developing reasoning and accepting some uncertainty. Discuss the difference between certain knowledge and a reasonably sound judgement, and how much it matters if we cannot be absolutely sure. In the absence of certain knowledge some students are inclined to think that all views are equally valuable/valueless and need to be encouraged to understand that a well-grounded, well-reasoned view has more value than a speculative or pre-judged view that does not use evidence well. Others are inclined to assert what they 'know'.

How do you know that?

Ask students to consider:

- which parts of the information given in the text are known, which are speculated, and which are interpretations supported by reasoning;
- the reliability of radiocarbon dating and why it matters to our judgement about Neanderthals whether this form of gaining evidence is reliable or not;
- the reliability of the different sources of information (newspaper, academics etc.) and how their reliability might affect our judgement;
- the degree of importance, when trying to form a judgement, of whether two different archaeological finds corroborate each other;
- how much evidence is necessary to change our view of Neanderthals.

Types of reasoning

- Is this passage an argument? Does it contain argument?
- What other sorts of reasoning does this passage contain?
- Why does it matter what sorts of reasoning are used?

- Who made the inference from 'sparkly pigment' to 'makeup', the scientists or the headline writers? How strong is this inference?
- To what extent is wearing makeup and jewellery evidence of intelligence? How much would your judgement differ if you were thinking about modern people rather than early humans?
- What if someone suggested that the pigment was war paint or used in rituals – would this affect your judgement about whether Neanderthals were the brutish halfwits that we imagine?
- Has the reasoning in the passage convinced you that there is 'absolutely no scientific justification to consider Neanderthals as the brutish halfwits they have been portrayed as in popular culture'? Why?
- Has the reasoning in the passage convinced you that Neanderthals were 'high minded'? Why?
- If there is a difference between your answers, why?

Comment
There are some comments on the companion website.

Presenting reasoning

You might ask students to engage in one or more of the following tasks.

- Research more evidence relating to Neanderthals. Produce a presentation putting forward a view on how sophisticated their thinking and culture were.
- 'To what extent can scientific standards of certainty be applied to history or archaeology?' Research evidence and write your own argument to support your view, using evidence.
- Research the reliability of radiocarbon and radiometric dating. Compare the strength of support given by scientists to the claim that these are reliable, and by creationists to the claim that these techniques are unreliable. Remember to focus on the support given, not on whether you agree with them.

Discussion: Difficulty

Do you think that Lesson Idea One or Two is more difficult? Why?

Donna's situation is simpler than the issue of gaining knowledge through archaeological evidence, but many of the thinking skills are similar. Making a decision about what to do in Donna's situation is not necessarily easier than forming a judgement about the sophistication of the Neanderthals. It would certainly be possible to think at a high level about an apparently simple, everyday situation, and at a low level about a more academic problem.

One of the challenges for the thinking teacher is to choose material that is accessible and interesting to students. Able students are inclined to be unhappy about exercising their thinking skills on very simple material, especially if they have not yet fully understood the focus on thinking and reasoning skills. On the other hand, choosing material that is too difficult in terms of content can make it difficult to develop and apply thinking and reasoning skills because students tend to be too involved with understanding issues. Many tend to focus on whether or not they agree with the ideas put forward rather than on the thinking and reasoning skills. So the thinking teacher needs to pitch the level of stimulus material carefully to the needs of their students, and manage the discussion of content versus development of skills through this discussion. We will discuss this at greater length in Chapter 5.

The Skills

In this chapter so far, the focus has been on using thinking and reasoning skills in order to ground beliefs, form judgements, make decisions and question knowledge. In many qualifications the skills are broken down into more easily manageable chunks, which can help students and teachers. However, it is very easy to lose track of what these isolated skills are for. It is important always to come back to the question, 'what are we doing this for?' Students who remember that the skills are being used for a purpose tend to apply them. This means that they not only write better essays, but also tend to write better answers in examinations focusing on thinking and reasoning skills. For example:

> Give and explain one weakness in the author's use of evidence to show that Neanderthals were more sophisticated than we generally believe.   [3 marks]

> Answer A: The author has used radiocarbon dating, which might not be 100 per cent reliable in this instance, as it works only on things that were once alive, and pigments in paints were never alive.

Answer B: The author has used radiocarbon dating, which works only on things that were once alive. The mineral pigments in the shell were never alive, *so* we can be sure only that the *shell* was around 50,000 years ago. It is possible that the pigments were added to an old shell much more recently. *So* we can't be sure that the Neanderthals made the pigment, *so* the conclusion that they were more sophisticated than we think is weakened.

Comment
Answer A has demonstrated the skill of spotting a weakness in the choice of evidence, but hasn't applied that skill to explaining why the weakness makes the author's case less strong. The answer would probably attract only one mark. Answer B has explained the weakness in relation to what the evidence was being used to show and given thought to the purpose of the evidence and of identifying the weakness of the evidence. This answer sets the skills firmly in context, and would probably attract all three marks.

Support

When we are trying to form judgements, ground beliefs and make decisions in a rational way, we put a lot of emphasis on reasoning which can support a conclusion. A judgement, belief or decision will be more solid and dependable (although not necessarily right) if it has rational support.

The support given to a conclusion is normally divided into two rough categories:

1. Evidence
2. (Structure of) reasoning

Evidence

Evidence generally refers to primary and secondary material used by an author (or speaker) to support their own reasoning. In its widest sense, evidence is a broad base of facts, figures, testimony, anecdotes, opinions and arguments. Evidence is used in this sense in court judgments, or when writing research reports. In its narrowest sense, evidence is facts, figures and statistics (used to support reasons) quoted in a report, explanation or argument.

The skills relating to evidence are:

- Assessing credibility and reliability. Is this a believable, trustworthy source of information? Should we be using it at all? Is there any corroboration of this evidence? Is this evidence plausible? How does the source get their information? In written examinations, students may have to make positive or negative comments about the credibility or reliability of a source of evidence. In essays or research reports, students should select reliable, credible sources to cite.
- Evaluating use of evidence to support a claim. Given that the evidence is both true and reliable, does it support the author's inferences/reasoning? Are there any weaknesses in the evidence/sources cited which would make us less likely to accept their conclusions?
- Making critical use of evidence to answer a question. This involves selecting appropriate evidence, weighing it, taking weakness in the evidence/sources into consideration, considering how much can be inferred from evidence, and using it to support one's own reasoning.

Structure of reasoning

The structure of reasoning relates to the logical structure of the writer's own reasoning. A student writing an essay should have a structure of reasoning, and use evidence to support it. A journalist might report on an incident, draw inferences from this, explain, introduce other ideas, and build up a structure of support for a conclusion. Evidence has an important role to play in this structure of reasoning, because it anchors the reasoning to real life (or reality), but it is a separate, supporting role.

Understanding the structure of reasoning, and being able to tell how strong reasoning is, are important skills in grounding our beliefs, forming judgements and making decisions both in everyday life and in academic work.

The skills relating to structure of reasoning are:[1]

- Identifying different kinds of reasoning, such as argument, explanation, rant (which is on the borderline of being reasoning).
- Identifying parts of reasoning, labelling them (as reasons, evidence, prediction, conclusion etc.) and showing how they fit together in a particular context.
- Evaluating strength and weakness in the structure of reasoning, by considering whether reasons really support conclusions, by

assessing the effect of any flaws (su
strength of support for a conclusion a
author has left unstated (but which in
or is an important step in the reasoning

- Developing reasoning with a structure (rat
opinion, or cutting and pasting).

Approaches to Teaching Thinking and Reasoning Skills

We are now going to think through a number of different issues relating to teaching thinking and reasoning skills, in order to help you develop strategies which work for you and your students. We will consider:

- independent learning;
- explicit and embedded skills teaching;
- explicit skills practice and practice in context;
- the role of the teacher.

Independent Learning

Most of the qualifications that emphasise thinking and reasoning skills also place a high value on students becoming independent thinkers and learners. Ideally, we would like our students to:

- Develop the skills to deal with the overwhelming flood of information available to them and be able to apply these skills without a teacher directing them (that is, to develop the tools to understand and shape their own world – with our assistance – rather than being passive recipients of our ideas about the world).
- Be able to work out what the issues are, what they need to know in order to make a judgement or decision, and how to go about discovering this information.
- Ideally, be able to frame their own research questions rather than waiting passively for a teacher to ask them a question.
- Research for themselves how the different perspectives on these issues are grounded, to *genuinely* engage with perspectives other than their own, and to consider whether their sources of information are reliable and well reasoned.
- Select appropriate information and use it to support their own reasoning.

- Be able to present information, ideas and arguments logically in a variety of formats, without us standing over them saying, 'Is it really appropriate to cut and paste your essay into a Powerpoint presentation?' That is, we would like our students to have and use thinking and reasoning skills.

In IGCSE Global Perspectives and Pre-U Global Perspectives and Independent Research Report, for example, this need for independence is clearly built into the syllabus and is reflected in the nature of the assessment. These qualifications include a high proportion of coursework, which students should carry out independently, using their thinking and reasoning skills. In qualifications fully assessed by written examination, such as GCE A Level Critical Thinking, the increasing need for independence is seen in the progression of question types. At AS level, questions tend to be focused and limited, whereas at A2 questions are more open and candidates are expected to select key issues to evaluate and to synthesise a number of skills.

Approaches to Independent Thinking

Students do not find independent thinking and learning easy. They need to be guided and nurtured towards independence, and the challenge for the thinking teacher is to provide sufficient guidance for students without providing so much that students do not have the space to develop their own skills.

Practice and modelling

Two of the key strategies for teaching and learning thinking skills are practising and modelling.

Like any other skill, thinking and reasoning skills need to be practised. Aspiring footballers do not get better only by sitting on the sofa watching the football coach playing football. They improve by practising, although it is of course beneficial to watch experts in addition to practising. Similarly, students will not improve if you do all the thinking. They can benefit by you modelling thinking skills, but will improve most by practising themselves.

Like any other skill, the student needs to be motivated and (to some extent) in control of their practice. A student who sees the point of improving their thinking and reasoning skills is likely to be fully engaged in practice as a meaningful activity, rather than as a meaningless repetition.

A student who has some measure of control over their progress is likely to be more actively engaged than one who has no control.

As with any other skill, there needs to be a balance between practising it to get better and practising it in context. Dribbling a ball is an important skill for the footballer to practise, but not an end in itself; it is useful only because of its application in a match. Similarly, assessing the credibility of sources is a useful skill to practise, but it is not an end in itself; it is useful only because of its more general application to research, belief and judgement formation and decision making.

This means that you will have to find the right balance between:

- explicit skill teaching and embedded skill teaching;
- practising skills explicitly and using skills in context;
- student and teacher control.

Explicit and Embedded Skill Teaching

Teaching skills explicitly means clearly and openly putting the emphasis on the skill to be learned, and making the skill the focus of your teaching. Embedded skill teaching means drawing out one or more skills whilst discussing a topic or area of interest. The focus here is on an issue, and the skills are seen very much as tools that are used to develop understanding of an issue. We will consider each in turn, and discuss ways of combining the methods.

Handouts A and B will be referred to in the lesson discussions that follow.

> ### Handout A
> Flaw in reasoning: a weakness in the structure of reasoning which means that the conclusion is not supported.
>
> ### Slippery slope
>
> Description: slippery slope is a flaw in reasoning in which a series of logical leaps is made, often involving the prediction of unlikely consequences, leading to an extreme conclusion.
>
> Example: *If I don't clean my windows soon they will be completely black, and I'll be locked away from the world. I'll never see people or sunshine again, and I'll become depressed and end up killing myself.*
>
> Explanation: almost every link in this reasoning is too extreme or exaggerated. Not cleaning the windows is unlikely to lead to them

continued

becoming completely black, and even if the windows are black, it is possible to open them, or to leave the house – it's not as if our only access to the world is through windows. So the final link in this chain is completely unsupported and we cannot accept the prediction of suicidal depression from the starting point of not cleaning the windows soon.

Post hoc

Description: Latin for 'after this'. This is a flaw in reasoning relating to the use of causal links. It can refer to any problem with cause and effect, such as an oversimplification of causes, a confusion of cause and effect, confusion of correlation and cause, or an attribution of a wrong cause. However, *post hoc* also has a narrower meaning, and is used to refer to the specific pattern of reasoning: 'A happened before B. Therefore A caused B.'

Example: *I was cleaning windows last week, and then I had a terrible migraine. I think cleaning windows gives me migraines, so I'd better not do that again.*

Explanation: this is *post hoc* reasoning in the narrow sense, assuming that cleaning windows causes migraines only on the basis that the window cleaning came before the migraine. However, to be sure of this link we would need a much more solid evidence base than one occurrence. We would need to consider what it is about cleaning windows that might cause a migraine – perhaps there is a chemical in the window cleaner that can cause migraines? But on the basis of a single instance of window cleaning happening before a migraine, it is not reasonable to conclude that, 'I'd better not do that again.'

Generalisation

Description: generalisation is moving from specific evidence to a general claim. Although generalisation does play an important role in scientific reasoning, it is important to ensure that there is sufficient high-quality evidence to support the generalisation. It is a flaw in reasoning if an author generalises from one to all, or draws sweeping, stereotypical generalisations.

Example (report in *Sports Gazette Monthly*): *A scientific research project has shown that teenagers concentrate better on practical, kinaesthetic tasks than on abstract, academic tasks. The study, which focused on a youth football team, included 20 males between the ages*

continued over

continued from over

of 14 and 16. The subjects were first taught three new ball skills and asked to practise them until they were competent. The average length of concentration was 15 minutes. The subjects were then given an IQ test. The average length of concentration was 5 minutes.

Explanation: This report generalises the results of the report from 20 male football players to teenagers generally. One small group like this is unlikely to be representative of teenagers generally. The report also generalises the study's findings from 'ball skills' to 'practical, kinaesthetic tasks'. Ball skills are only one kind of practical, kinaesthetic task, and a youth football team is likely to be particularly interested in improving their ball skills, and would therefore concentrate on them for longer than other tasks. Equally, the report generalises from IQ tests to 'abstract, academic tasks' in general. IQ tests are not the most engaging of abstract tasks. So there are many reasons why we can't accept the conclusion that 'teenagers concentrate better on practical, kinaesthetic tasks than on abstract, academic tasks', on the basis of this evidence.

Handout B

We have very sensitive brains which respond to minute changes in our environment. Our children's environment has changed dramatically in the past generation. They are now surrounded by all sorts of electronic gadgets. These gadgets respond immediately, which means that children are not learning the concept of a long, slow effort leading to a reward, so they are not learning any kind of self-control at all. They expect instant rewards. This will inevitably lead to increased crime and the inability to submit to a working environment. Why work for a living when you can hit an old lady and run off with her money? Our morality is in desperate danger because of these gadgets.

Children multi-task on these gadgets, so they are losing the ability to concentrate on a single task, which means they are less efficient. My daughter was doing her French homework whilst listening to rap music and updating her status on Facebook. Obviously, her homework was full of grammatical errors. It's not surprising that this multi-tasking is leading to a decline in educational standards, which the Government is trying to hide by handing out top-grade A Levels with NHS treatment. Some might try to persuade us that being able to cope with multiple sources of information is a useful skill in the modern world, but these are the sort of irresponsible people who brought about a near financial collapse in 2008. We must protect our future from the threats posed by gadgets to our children's brains.

continued

continued

Read the text about electronic gadgets. Find three flaws in the reasoning, and explain why they mean that the reasoning does not fully support the conclusion: 'We must protect our future from the threats posed by gadgets to our children's brains.'

1. Name and description of flaw and explanation of why the flaw means the reasoning does not support the conclusion: ....
    ....
    ....

2. Name and description of flaw and explanation of why the flaw means the reasoning does not support the conclusion: ....
    ....
    ....

3. Name and description of flaw and explanation of why the flaw means the reasoning does not support the conclusion: ....
    ....
    ....

Explicit skill teaching

Let's look at a lesson that uses explicit skill teaching.

Lesson A

Aim: All should be able to recognise three common flaws in reasoning: slippery slope, generalisation, and causal problems (*post hoc*), and most should be able to explain why these flaws weaken the reasoning.

Means: Defining and giving examples of flaws. Exercises, games.

Teacher: *Today we are going to consider flaws in reasoning. A flaw in reasoning is a weakness in the structure of the reasoning. You can think of it like a building; you can use the same bricks, but one way of putting them together makes a strong building which stands up, and another way makes a weak building which does not stand up.* (The teacher might demonstrate this with children's building blocks, or images.) *It's similar when you organise ideas into an argument. Some structures are stronger than others.*

The teacher could distribute Handout A (above and online) and talk through it. Alternatively, the handout could be made into nine laminated cards. Each card should have a description, an example or an explanation of a particular flaw in reasoning. Students should then move round the room to find the other students whose cards complete the set. This gets students moving, which can promote thinking, and means that they have to read the cards in order to complete their task.

Once students have found their partners, they can read out their cards or explain in their own words why the reasoning means that the conclusion is only weakly supported. Alternatively, able students could be challenged to think up another example of reasoning that is flawed in the same way as the reasoning on their cards. Once students have shared their new understanding, all students should be given Handout A for reference.

The teacher could then distribute Handout B (see above and online) and ask students to complete the activity in pairs or small groups. After the task, discuss students' answers and how they could improve them, remembering to focus on the explanations; merely naming and describing flaws is a low-level skill.

Advantages of explicit skills teaching:

- The teacher can prepare for everything and be in control.
- The teacher is sure that students have covered necessary skills.
- Students are encouraged to use a framework that will help them access high marks in an examination.
- There is a clarity to this form of teaching which should help students to structure their understanding.
- Students gain the language to discuss their thinking.
- Students develop a metacognitive approach – a way of thinking and talking about their own thinking, which is a valuable tool for improving their thinking.

Disadvantages of explicit skills teaching:

- Students are more or less limited to what the teacher has thought; there is little opportunity for them to articulate their own understandings.
- It can seem as if the skills are something that the teacher 'owns' and has control of.
- The skills can be divorced from their real purpose if this form of teaching is overused.
- Students can become alienated or disengaged if this type of teaching dominates. They are likely to think of it as 'boring and pointless'.

Embedded skill teaching

Let's look at a lesson that uses embedded skill teaching.

Lesson B

Context: Students are working on a project on education, discussing whether technology is useful as an educational tool. In a previous lesson, students have discussed the issue and identified many benefits.

Aims: To explore the perspective that technology can have negative effects on young people and build up the broader context of the debate. To revisit the evaluation of, use of, and response to other people's arguments.

Means: Discussion, questioning, response to students.

Teacher: *We talked yesterday about the benefits of technology in education and for young people's development. Before we start researching in groups, we're going to consider a different perspective and think about how we can assess and use other people's reasoning.*

The teacher hands out page 1 of Handout B and asks students to read the article. Alternatively, the teacher might give students a task to complete using the handout, which would revise a previously covered skill or focus on the qualities of this particular article. For example, the students could underline any argument indicator words (such as so, therefore, because), or highlight any predicted consequences, or use different colours to underline facts, opinions, values etc., or indicate which parts of the text they accept and which they do not.

Once the students have familiarised themselves with the text, ask: 'What do you think of this?' Note the open question, with emphasis on what the students think.

> **Student A:** *It's rubbish. It's written by some old person who's scared of gadgets they don't know how to use.*
> **Teacher:** *What makes you think that?*
> **Student A:** *It predicts all sorts of doom-and-gloom consequences, and they're just not going to happen, are they? Listening to your iPod isn't going to make you a criminal.*
> **Student B:** *I agree. The author's predicting lots of unlikely consequences. It just doesn't seem logical that using electronic gadgets could lead to moral depravity, or huge dangers, or inability to learn. Maybe we just learn in different ways.*

continued over

continued from over

Teacher: *So you think that the author is being illogical? That's interesting. There is a name for this long train of illogical leaps and unlikely consequences. It's 'slippery slope reasoning'. Because the author leaps from one thing to the next without logical connection, their conclusion ends up being unsupported. In this case that means that we don't have to accept that 'Our morality is in desperate danger because of these gadgets', and this really weakens the support for the conclusion that 'We must protect our future from the threats posed by gadgets to our children's brains', because if there isn't such a desperate danger, there isn't such a need to protect children.*

Student A: *So we're not just disagreeing; we can say, 'You haven't supported your conclusion very well.' So we have a reason.*

Teacher: *Something like that, yes.*

Student C: *But what about cyber bullying? Isn't there some evidence that even nice people will say horrible things on Facebook because they can't see the other person? So electronic things might have some effect on morality.*

Teacher: *There's two points here. One is that a slippery slope often takes a small thing that seems reasonable, and blows it up into something extreme and unreasonable. The other is that you are doing the reasoning the author ought to have done. The author's reasoning here doesn't support their conclusions. That doesn't mean that the conclusions are completely wrong, just that they are unsupported. We have to do some thinking and take the evidence into consideration before we make our own judgement.* [Talks through slippery slope with another example.] [Discussion not recorded here ...]

Student C: *The author implies that her daughter made mistakes in her French homework because she was doing other things. I can see that there might be some truth in that, but what if she's just not very good at French, or if her French teacher isn't very good? Perhaps her French homework would have been full of grammatical mistakes anyway. Mine always is, however hard I concentrate. So I don't think it's very reasonable to say that all the educational decline is because of gadgets.*

Teacher: *So you think that she's oversimplifying the causes and effects, as well as making completely illogical leaps. Yes. That's a really common pattern of flawed reasoning too.* [Teacher talks through *post hoc* flaw with another example.] [Explanation not recorded here...].

Student D: *Can I ask something? I can see that it's illogical to think that A causes B just because A happens before B. But isn't it sometimes a useful way of thinking? Might we have evolved to think like that?*

continued

continued

Teacher: *What do you mean?*

Student D: *Well, if you think about primitive people, you don't want to take too long to make the connection between irritating tigers or wolves and getting eaten. So sometimes it might be good to be illogical.*

Student C: *Maybe, but what if we've also evolved to be rational, so that we can correct our first impulses. So we have the first response which might save our lives, and then we can sit and think about things and use reason and logic.*

Teacher: *That sounds plausible. Maybe you two could do some research into evolutionary theory? You could give a presentation at our seminar next month if you're interested. Coming back to education, can anyone see anything about this text that is plausible, or that you might accept?*

Student E: *I think it might be reasonable to say that 'We have very sensitive brains which respond to minute changes in our environment.' And I don't think it's wrong to say that we have learned to expect instant reactions. But I don't think the author has given us enough evidence to accept it.*

Teacher: *Yes, they are interesting ideas, but the author has just asserted them. Would you like to investigate and find out if there are any experiments or research that have been done to support these claims? Remember to check the credibility of your sources, and check the quality of the reasoning in anything you read.* [... **teacher continues discussion, covers generalisation ...**]

Teacher distributes Handout A.

Teacher: *Let's reinforce this thinking about weak patterns of reasoning. Work in pairs or threes to add notes from our discussion today about each of these flaws. See if you can remember as much as possible, and try to focus on the things we said about patterns of reasoning, and why flaws in someone's reasoning might make you think twice about using their work to support your own argument.'*

Students write notes on handouts. Teacher distributes Handout B page 2 and asks students to complete it for homework, and look out for any other weaknesses in the reasoning (which may have emerged in the lesson).

Teacher: *For the rest of the lesson we're going to consider what other perspectives there might be on the issue of technology in education. Can anyone suggest anything?*

continued over

continued from over

Student F: *People in countries where there isn't such good access to technology might have a different perspective. For example in Swaziland schools only have limited access to the internet.*
Teacher: *So? How might this affect their perspective? [...]*

Next lesson

Students work in groups to set research questions in this area, with teacher assistance, before beginning to research and put an argument together for a presentation. The teacher reminds students to consider the credibility of sources and strength of reasoning before using a source of information to support their own reasoning.

Advantages of embedded skills teaching:

- This approach really allows students to see the skills used in context, for a real purpose. It can therefore seem more meaningful to students than abstracting the skills from the context.
- This approach makes it easier for students to apply their thinking and reasoning skills.
- Students are often more engaged with this approach to learning skills.
- The teacher is really interacting with students and with their thinking.
- The students can be encouraged to develop their thinking from their existing base.
- Students have more control and ownership of their learning.

Disadvantages of embedded skills teaching:

- This approach can be quite tricky to manage.
- It is possible for students to sidetrack the teacher. This may be beneficial (or not!), but it does mean that different groups have different learning experiences.
- The teacher must always be on the ball and responsive, and this can be both intense and tiring.
- It can be harder to keep an overview of which skills have been covered.
- Students can ask questions to which the teacher does not know the answer, which can be unsettling. However, these can be batted back to students by asking what they think, or asking someone to research the information.

Discussion

What balance of explicit and embedded skills teaching will best suit you, your students and the qualification you are working on? How much explicit teaching should you do if your qualification is predominantly coursework? How much embedded teaching should you do if your qualification is predominantly assessed by written examination?

You might find it useful to keep a space in your log book or professional journal to record your ongoing thoughts about the discussions. You can record your experiments with new ways of teaching. Make sure you write about the things that went well. It is sometimes tempting to make too much of the difficulties we encounter. You may find that you are initially happier with either explicit or embedded teaching, but that as you try different strategies and combine the approaches, your feelings change.

What's in a name?

How much does it matter whether students can name specific flaws in reasoning?

Naming flaws can be useful as a way of learning how to recognise a problematic pattern of reasoning. However, knowing the name of a flaw in itself is insufficient to demonstrate that a student truly understands why and to what extent the reasoning is weak. It is important always to encourage students to explain a weakness, not just to name it. You can do this by asking, 'Why does that matter?' or 'How much does that weaken the argument?' or 'Does that mean that you don't accept the author's conclusion?' or 'Has the author provided any other reasoning that supports the conclusion, even though that part of the reasoning is weak?'

Practising Skills Explicitly and Using Skills in Context

Many of the issues relating to practising skills explicitly and using skills in context are similar to the issue relating to teaching these skills in an implicit or embedded way. As with the young footballer, the key is to get the right balance between practising skills explicitly in order to do them better, and practising them in a meaningful context. Let's look briefly at different ways of practising evaluating the quality of source material.

Lesson C

The teacher provides two different documents and tells the class that they are going to assess the credibility of the documents. The teacher displays the following:

> The credibility of Document X / Person Y / Claim Z is strengthened/weakened by … (insert criterion) … because … (insert explanation).

The teacher asks questions such as:

1. How credible is Document 1?
2. How credible is Dr Y?
3. How credible is Dr Y's claim '…'?

Students answer the questions orally or in writing, as follows:

> The credibility of Document 1 which comes from Publication X is strengthened by its reputation as a newspaper that employs expert journalists and checks its facts, because this means that it is unlikely to include incorrect facts.

Lesson D

The class agrees on a research question and each group of students brings a selection of sources of evidence (in the broadest sense of the word) to the next lesson. The teacher selects two of these sources for class evaluation.

> **Teacher:** *So, we have a report from Oxfam. Overall, do you think this is a reliable source of information to use?*
> **Student A:** *Well, they're a charity, so they're not going to lie, are they? I'd say they were quite reliable.*
> **Teacher:** *What's the purpose of the report?*
> **Student B:** *They're using that report to show how bad conditions are for people in Afghanistan, and how we should oppose the current militarised aid strategy, and they want people to donate money.[2] So I suppose they might have a vested interest to exaggerate to make us donate more, but it looks to me like a serious report put together by experts. I don't think I agree with their conclusions, but I think the facts are probably reliable.*

continued

continued

Teacher: *That's really good. It's important to distinguish between the specific evidence and the conclusions that are drawn from it. So, would you use this report as a reliable source?*

[the discussion continues ...]

Teacher: *We also have some information from Wikipedia. Overall, do you think this is a reliable source of information to use?*

Student A: *No. Anyone can change the content, so it could be completely wrong. You don't have to know anything to change Wiki.*

Student B: *But if someone puts something inaccurate or doesn't quote sources, someone else will change it so that it's correct. So I don't think it's all that inaccurate.*

Student A: *But what if they change it to something else that's inaccurate? Or if someone deliberately changes it to be wrong? And if the person who makes an entry has a bias, we might never know.*

Teacher: *So do these issues about expertise and access to accurate information mean that you shouldn't use Wikipedia as a source of knowledge or information?*

Student B: *I don't think so. But perhaps we should only use it as a starting point, and make sure that we check the facts with other sources.*

Teacher: *That's another really important point.* **[Talks about corroboration and consistency]**

Lesson E

Students are engaged in independent study towards a presentation or essay. The teacher schedules a five-minute meeting with each student to discuss their sources and progress.

Teacher: *You seem to be relying very heavily in your thinking on this blog. Why have you chosen this document? ... Do you think that this is a credible source of information?*

Student: *I know the blog is a bit extreme, and the author doesn't seem to have any kind of expertise, so I don't think that it's a credible source of information, but I do think that it represents what a lot of people think. I wanted to explore their perspective more deeply.*

Teacher: *Are there other sources out there that would broaden your evidence base a bit? It would be a bit harsh to reject the whole perspective because of one dodgy blog, wouldn't it?*

continued over

continued from over

> **Student:** *I did find this article from a journal. It looks like a proper academic study, so I think it's more credible. But it's from 1988, so I'm not really sure it's fully relevant. I'm starting to wonder whether I ought to change my focus.*
>
> **Teacher:** *Well, let's think about how you're searching, first, and if there really isn't enough reliable material, you might have to rethink. Perhaps changing your search terms would help?*

Lesson C is very clear, and gives students a structure which they can learn and practise. However, it does not fully apply this understanding to a context in which discussing credibility is purposeful. Lessons D and E do not emphasise the same clear structure, but they do put very much more focus on using the skill of assessing the credibility of a source for a purpose. These two options also give students much more ownership of the skill than Lesson C.

Discussion

How much of a role is there for explicit skills practice such as Lesson C in a course that is tested primarily by coursework? How much of a role is there for practising skills in context, such as Lessons D or E, in a course that is tested predominantly by written examination? How much could you tweak the approaches as shown above? Could Lesson C be altered so that, in addition to clarity of structure, students also gained an understanding of the application of the skill they are practising? Could Lesson D be tweaked to encourage students to articulate more clearly their assessment of the credibility of the sources without losing their ownership of the skill?

The Role of the Teacher

Whether thinking skills are taught and practised explicitly or embedded in a context, teaching thinking and reasoning skills can place different demands on the teacher from their primary subject. Because the focus is firmly on what students can *do* rather than on what they *know*, there is less need for the teacher to stand at the front of the class and share information than in traditional subjects.

Because of the need for greater student independence in developing their own skills, the teacher may need to hand over some control to students. For example, if your aim is to improve their research skills (so that they select appropriate, relevant and reliable sources, and use information to support their own reasoning rather than copying and pasting), you might give them control of their own topics. This may mean that you are helping them to develop skills in an area in which the student knows more than you. This can make you feel insecure, especially if you are most used to directing lessons from the front and being 'the expert'. However, it is important to remember that the internet has made information readily accessible. The teacher is in any case no longer the guardian of and point of access to knowledge. The role has changed, with much more emphasis placed now on enabling young people to cope with the information that is available.

Discussion
It can be very uncomfortable teaching in unfamiliar ways, especially if you are still finding your way with thinking and reasoning skills. Think about your main subject teaching. You probably use a great many different strategies to motivate students and encourage them to engage in learning. Which of these could be applied to teaching thinking and reasoning skills? Are there strategies you use which could be adapted or tweaked to emphasise the thinking and reasoning skills that students are developing?

In the early stages of most courses the teacher will typically lead lessons. In many, especially those that require a great deal of student independence, the teacher will gradually step back and allow students to lead. For example, in early lessons, the teacher is likely to determine the topic, texts and skills. By the end of most courses, students ought to be able to determine the topic, set a question, research their own information, and apply skills developed earlier in the course. They may be able to say to you, 'I'm having trouble with X; can you help me?' At this stage, students may lead seminars and evaluate each other's work. This does not mean that the teacher is redundant. The students might control their own work and learning, but the teacher controls the learning environment. This involves a number of different strategies. We will revisit some of these ideas in Chapter 4 when we consider lesson planning.

Judge and plan

As a teacher you have a very strong role in planning students' gradual progress to independence and handing them control of their learning when you judge the time is right. This involves allowing yourself, and the students, to make mistakes. After a difficult early attempt to allow some independence, it can be tempting to think, 'Oh well, that didn't work, I won't do that again.' But it may be that you need only to make minor adjustments to turn what felt like a disaster into a successful lesson. For example, if students did not understand what they were supposed to be doing, you could ask, 'How can I set our next lesson up more clearly, so that they do understand?' If students didn't manage to apply their thinking skills to the context, and just copied and pasted from an online encyclopaedia, perhaps ask yourself, 'How can I encourage students to use their skills next time? Do I need to adjust my focus? Do I need to model for them what they should be doing? Do I need to walk around and talk to students about their work more? How can I support them better so that they can work independently?'

Organise and manage

Even with the most independent students there is still a need for an organising mind to have an overview, and to guide students towards desired outcomes. Students are likely to plan their work around topics and in response to what interests them. It is a very unusual student who remains fully focused on the skills in the Assessment Objectives, for example. So the thinking teacher will need to organise and manage progress. This can include setting up independent work within a framework, reminding students what they need to achieve, and questioning students to prod them towards the right sort of outcome.

Enable

The teacher will need to enable students to work independently. This can mean organising rooms and equipment and setting clear time frames and goals. It can mean being there to answer questions when there are difficulties, making suggestions or helping students to clarify their ideas through discussion. It can also mean revising skills, helping students to apply them in context and extend them to deal with more challenging contexts. One method of enabling students is by helping them frame research questions in ways that use their thinking and reasoning skills and are likely to lead to strong outcomes. We will talk more about this in Chapters 3 and 4.

Motivate

Many students will need you to motivate them to work independently, especially when they are struggling, or when there is time pressure from other subjects. You may have to encourage them to find their interests, spark new ideas, show them the progress they have made to reassure them they are getting better, and make it clear that everyone contributes to team efforts. Games and competitions can be a good motivator. (See Chapter 4 for some games ideas.)

Support

While students are working independently you have a valuable opportunity to talk to them individually, to find out about their individual strengths and weaknesses, their likes and dislikes, and their interests. This gives you the opportunity to support, reassure and encourage them. It also allows you to respond to and ask questions, giving students the opportunity to use you as a sounding board.

Create confidence

One way of creating an environment in which students have the confidence to take control is by creating an atmosphere in which there are no right or wrong answers, and in which it is acceptable to make mistakes. In traditional subjects many students feel inhibited because the 'answer' is something that exists outside of them, known by the teacher and 'clever' children. In thinking and reasoning skills, there is no right answer, there are only better and worse ways of answering questions.

Many weaker students flourish when they realise that what they think matters and is not going be dismissed as 'wrong'. More able students need to push themselves beyond their comfort zone, for exactly the opposite reason: they are used to being 'right'. One way of achieving this is to always ask 'Why?' whenever a student ventures an opinion. Another is to ask unusual questions, such as 'Is the gap between the notes music?'[3] or 'Is there more happiness or sadness in the world?'[4] Follow up by adding more questions, such as, 'Why?' or 'How do you know?' or by suggesting a counterargument and expecting students to answer it. Knowing there isn't a single right answer can give students confidence to explore their ideas.

Another way to create an environment in which students are sufficiently confident to take control of their own learning is by changing the traditional boundaries between teacher and student. Much of this can be done through classroom layout. Many teachers already have students seated around tables or in a horseshoe rather than in rows. Consider also where you stand or sit; are you always at the front? What would happen if you talked to students from the back of the room? Is there a barrier between you and students?

Assess

In many cases you will also be an assessor, having a formative role in assessing students' progress and helping them to set goals for further advances. If you are marking students' coursework, this will give you an insight into how the assessment works, which you can share with students to empower them. Show them generic mark schemes and discuss with them what they need to do to move their work up to the next level.

Question

Asking questions is one of the most valuable tools you have as a thinking teacher. Questions engage your students actively in a thinking process; answers leave students passive. Another reason to ask questions rather than give answers is to keep students' options open. Telling them the answer can be very limiting, and can shut down profitable avenues of thought.

Of all questions, the most valuable is probably 'Why?' because it makes students think, see connections, draw inferences, consider support, chase ideas and start to justify their own views. If your normal response to a student expressing a view is to ask 'Why?', students understand that everyone is being treated equally; they are not being marked as 'right' or 'wrong', just prompted to think more deeply.

What colour are your questions?

Generally speaking, asking open questions allows students to develop their thinking and reasoning skills. But not all questions are equal. Bloom's Revised Taxonomy of thinking skills is a useful aid to question formation.[5]

Bloom drew up a diagram of thinking skills in a pyramid with higher level thinking skills at the top, as follows:

- **Creating** (synthesizing), coloured yellow on the diagram;
- **Evaluating**, coloured blue on the diagram;
- **Analysing**, coloured green on the diagram;
- **Applying**, coloured purple on the diagram;
- **Understanding**, coloured red on the diagram;
- **Remembering**, coloured orange on the diagram.

The skills at the top depend upon those at the bottom. It is difficult for a student to evaluate (give value to, or make a judgement about) an issue which she does not understand. It is difficult to analyse an issue or argument (break it down into its parts and understand their relationship to one another) if the student knows or remembers nothing about the issue. You may wish to follow the link on the website to see the diagram.

All of these skills have some value, but the skills at the top of the pyramid are the higher-level skills. Level 3 qualifications in thinking and reasoning tend to award marks only for the top three skills: analysing, evaluating and creating (which involves synthesising a number of skills in order to develop a reasoned argument that makes evaluative use of evidence). This means that your questions need to prompt students to think in ways that will result in high-level thinking. Generally speaking, open questions with no fixed answer are more likely to prompt students to use their higher-level thinking skills than closed questions with a right answer already known to the teacher. Let's consider some specific questions.

What is the flaw in this reasoning?
This is a closed question – the answer to which might be 'slippery slope' – asking students to remember a pattern of reasoning and recognise it in a new context. Designed to test fairly low-level skills – at best, elements of understanding and applying, but probably mostly remembering – it could be described as orangey-red. The question has its place in the thinking classroom, because students need to remember and recognise problematic reasoning as a step towards evaluating weakness. Learning about specific flaws can help candidates to go beyond a counter-argument or disagreement with the evidence and begin to evaluate the strength of the reasoning. However, to really prompt analytic, evaluative and creative (synthetic) thinking, this question must be followed by a more open question.

Why is this flaw in the reasoning a problem?

The answer here might be: 'The author leaps from a small problem (cannabis smoking) to extreme consequences unsupported by logic (heroin addiction, crime, death in the gutter, social decline), and these consequences are far too extreme. The link between smoking cannabis and heroin addiction is far less strong than the author implies, and even heroin addiction doesn't necessarily lead to the dire consequences the author predicts. So we can't accept the author's view that cannabis smoking is a serious problem.' This more open question asks students to explain, asking for understanding with a little application, so we could describe it as reddish purple.

To what extent does this flaw weaken the reasoning?

The answer to this question might be: 'Because the author's reasoning relies on extreme consequences that are unlikely to come about (slippery slope from smoking cannabis through heroin addiction and death to social decline); the author has not supported their intermediate conclusion that "smoking cannabis is a serious social ill". The main conclusion, "The law should therefore punish cannabis smoking more strictly", relies very heavily on this intermediate conclusion – there would be very little reason to punish cannabis smoking more strictly if it was not a serious social ill – so this flaw weakens the support for the main conclusion to a great extent.' The question is an open one, asking students to evaluate and justify (create), and as such can be seen as blue, with a little yellow.

So, would you use this argument as source material? Why (not)?

The answer to these questions might be: 'No, I'm looking for a stronger argument that gives much better reasons for punishing cannabis use more strictly.' Or, alternatively: 'Yes, I might, it's a good starting point. I'm going to see if I can find some evidence to support some of these claims – this isn't a very good article, but I want to see if there is any better reasoning or scientific evidence I could use.' This, then, is an open question focusing on the very highest skills – using evaluation of source material to create one's own reasoning. We can describe it as yellow.

A word of warning about 'Why?'

'Why?' can be one of your most useful tools, really encouraging students to think and to justify their reasoning; that is, it can encourage students to synthesise their other skills and create their own reasoning. However, 'Why?' can also be used to prompt students to remember learned material. Let's look at the difference between the two uses.

Why did the 13 American colonies declare their independence from Britain?

This question is orangey-red; it prompts students to give an explanation, one they have probably learned, with the teacher expecting certain responses. That is, it asks students to remember, and perhaps to understand. The focus of the question is on the information rather than on manipulating that information for a purpose using thinking and reasoning skills.

Why do you think that religion is more important than science?

This question is yellow with touches of blue and green; it prompts students to argue and justify. To answer it well the student will need to shape their own ideas, and make critical use of evidence. The focus here is on analysis, evaluation and creation of reasoning.

Task 1

Re-read Lessons A–E above. What different strategies are the teachers using? How effective do you think they are? Use your log book to make notes and reflect on any ideas you have for improving your own practice.

Task 2

Record one of your own lessons. You could use a microphone for audio recording, or a webcam or video recorder so that you can see your body language and movements around the classroom.

Focus on the questions you ask.

a) How many questions do you ask?
b) Do you sometimes give answers when a question would be better?
c) What colour are your questions? Take a piece of paper (squared paper or graph paper is good) and six coloured pens. Each square on the paper represents a question. Colour a square orange every time you ask a question that relates to remembering. Colour a square red every time you ask one about understanding, and so on. If your question addresses two or more skills, colour the square in two or more colours.
d) Overall, what colour is your lesson?
e) Now review your lesson aims. Does the colour of your questions match the colour of your aims? For example, if your aim was to develop students' evaluative skills, and you have a lot of blue squares, then

your questions are likely to help students evaluate, and your aims to be met. On the other hand, if your aim was to develop evaluative skills, but you have a lot of orange and red squares, then your questions are unlikely to help students to evaluate.

f) How could you improve on this lesson for next time? Use your log book to reflect on what you have learned from this activity.

Adapting this task

This task can be adapted for other aims. You could focus on how much you are talking versus how much students are talking, or on how much you give answers rather than ask questions. You could concentrate on how you use space in the classroom, or on getting a different angle on how students work together while you are walking round the class. Perhaps consider the different roles you take on during a lesson – enabler, manager, questioner, assessor. If you are too busy to watch a whole lesson, why not select a ten-minute slot, or maybe ask a colleague to observe your teaching in this way?

3   Planning a Course

Whether you are a subject coordinator, a single-teacher department, or a teacher within a bigger department, you are likely to need to make some decisions about course planning. In this chapter, we discuss some of the issues that confront a course planner, and look at different ways of organising courses. As elsewhere, the aim is to raise issues and make suggestions rather than provide complete solutions. The thinking course planner will need to select and adapt ideas and apply them to the specific circumstances in their own school. As many of the courses include common aims and thinking skills, the thinking teacher will gain useful ideas from considering learning models and course planning from other qualifications.

The fundamental questions when planning a course are:

- What do students need to be able to do in order to pass the exam?
- When do they need to be able to do this by?
- What is the best way of making sure that students are as well prepared as possible to do well in the exam?

What do Students Need to be Able to Do in Order to Pass the Exam?

It goes without saying that the thinking course planner will use the current syllabus or specification and recent exam papers and mark scheme to work out what should be tested and how this is usually done. This should give the thinking course planner the basic building blocks of the course – the question, as we shall see below, is how to structure these into a successful course that meets its aims.

When do They Need to be Able to Do this By?

Here the course planner must consider whether the course is linear or modular, when coursework or independent research needs to be completed, and how long students will need to reach the level of independent thinking skills required to produce high-quality work.

Linear

If the course is fully linear, the course planner's life is somewhat simplified, as all written examinations and coursework come, or are due, at the end of the course. There is the question of when students should do coursework. Here the course planner needs to consider optimum timing, when students have developed the confidence to work independently, but not leaving the work too late.

IGCSE Global Perspectives, for example, is fully linear, with all work due to be handed in at the end of the course. A portfolio and project need to be completed in addition to a written examination. Should students begin examined work in the first year? If so, at what point? Should they spend the first year building up skills, exploring topics and gradually becoming sufficiently independent to do assessed work in the second year? Is it too much for students to do all of the assessed work in the second year? In a fully linear course, the course planner needs to consider when and how to schedule revision of those skills or topics covered early in the course.

Modular

In a modular course, such as GCE A Level Critical Thinking, the course planner has a number of options. It is possible to:

- enter candidates for all exams at the end of the two-year course;
- enter candidates for AS exams at the end of the first year of the course and A2 exams at the end of the second;
- enter candidates for modules in January and June, or May and November (depending on which hemisphere you live in) in both the first and second years of the course.

In a content-based assessment, it might make sense for students to take modules in every possible exam session. This arrangement means that students do not need to remember as much at any one time as they do in a linear exam, and do not have too many exams at any one time, spreading the load. On the other hand, ongoing exam stress and pressure to perform may detract from a student's ability to learn at their own pace, develop skills and allow themselves to make mistakes. Furthermore, even a few months' additional maturity can improve students' ability to use and apply thinking and reasoning skills.

The thinking course planner needs to consider that skills are remembered and developed differently from information, so the case for modules in every exam session differs for qualifications involving thinking and reasoning skills. There is still a case – especially for weaker students – for taking modules separately, so that students can keep skills and tasks clear in their minds. However, the first exam session is very close to the beginning of a two-year course, which does not give students much time to develop.

To a certain extent, school policy will determine when exams are taken. Where the course planner has freedom to decide, a further consideration is the effect that exam timing can have on the overall planning. An integrated model of repetition and gradual progression might fit more naturally with infrequent examinations than with frequent.

Mixed linear/modular

Pre-U Global Perspectives and Independent Research Report (GPR) perhaps stands alone in its mixture of linear and modular approaches. The three papers that make up Global Perspectives are designed to equip students with the skills they need for the Independent Research Report. It is therefore possible to take the three Global Perspectives papers before submission of the Independent Research Report. Global Perspectives can be taken in the examination session at the end of the first year (May/June in the northern hemisphere; November in the southern); in the examination session at the beginning of the second year (November; or May/June); or in the final examination session at the same time as submission of the Independent Research Report. However, if students wish to re-sit, they must re-sit all of the examinations. It is not possible to re-sit a single paper.

The course planner therefore has to consider which model will best allow students to be successful in the three Global Perspectives papers, whilst also giving them time to complete the Independent Research Report. Another consideration is avoiding clashes with coursework for other subjects.

Independent research

A further consideration is planning for independent learning and study. If students have to complete a major piece of coursework, independent study or research report in the second year of a qualification, a framework enabling them to work independently needs to be largely in place by the end of the first year. Students will need to have developed:

- the ability to set (or negotiate with the teacher) a question that will allow them to meet the Assessment Objectives;
- research skills, including the ability to find and evaluate the

credibility, relevance and usefulness of sources;

- the ability to assess reasoning (at least to some extent);
- the confidence to express their own views and seek advice appropriately;
- the ability to develop reasoning that makes critical use of evidence in a way appropriate to their chosen field of study;
- an understanding of what they are aiming to achieve in their independent study.

The thinking course planner will need to consider when and how these skills are to be developed during the first year of the course. It may also be necessary to schedule some individual meetings between students and teacher or tutor to negotiate topics and titles, and to plan in some lessons in which students evaluate each other's proposals. This may mean that other parts of the course are pushed back into the second year.

Skills development

A further question for consideration when laying out the basic building blocks of the course is the way in which students develop their thinking skills. Watch your students. Do they develop a similar amount each week, so that by January they are about half as good as they will be in May? Do they have spurts of insight and progress, followed by periods in which they consolidate the insight, fall into self-doubt or seem to stagnate? Do they forget by June what was covered in January? Do they spend the first five months of the course rebelling and wondering what the point is, before suddenly understanding what it's all about just before the exam?

Keep notes for yourself in your log book about how students' thinking develops. How can you adapt your course to take your students' development into consideration?

Discussion

How much choice do you have about when exams are taken? What are the advantages and disadvantages in your school of each option available to you? What decision are you likely to make? How is the principal or head teacher likely to respond if you make a case for an option different from the norm in school? What effect do you think the timing of exams is likely to have on your other decisions? Revisit these thoughts when you have finished the chapter. How different is your thinking?

What is the Best Way of Making Sure that Students are as Well Prepared as Possible to Do Well in the Exam?

A major decision when considering how best to prepare students for the course is what mixture of explicit and embedded teaching and practice will best suit you, your students and the qualification you are working on. See Chapter 2 for a detailed discussion of the advantages and disadvantages of different approaches to teaching thinking skills.

The mixture of explicit and embedded skills teaching may well be reflected in the way you structure your course around skills or topic areas. In this section, we are going to consider what these approaches mean in terms of planning, and how they can be combined and adapted. We will also consider the need to build in gradual progression towards independent thinking.

Note that all options are suggestions only, to help inform thinking; none is intended to represent the 'right' answer.

Structure around skills

One option when planning the course is to take the skills from the syllabus or specification, and block them against weeks.

OCR AS Critical Thinking: Unit 1, 'Introduction to Critical Thinking' to be taken in January

> Week One: Identifying arguments (differentiating from dispute, report, explanation etc).
> Week Two: Identifying conclusions and reasons.
> Week Three: How reasons support conclusions.
> Week Four: Supporting reasoning with evidence and examples.
> Week Five: Argument and counter-argument.
> Week Six: Analysing more complex arguments into reasons, conclusion, evidence, example, counter-argument.
> Week Seven: Evaluating collection of evidence - sampling, representativeness, questionnaires etc.
> Week Eight: Half term.
> Week Nine: Credibility of sources and documents
> Week Ten: Credibility of individuals and specific claims
> Week Eleven: Images
> Week Twelve: Plausibility and likelihood

Week Thirteen: Making a judgement
Week Fourteen: Exam practice
Holiday
Exam.

This model ensures that students have covered the required skills, but it doesn't guarantee they will see the point and application of them, or remember those they learnt early. This approach can be effective but also seem rather joyless. The planner will probably need to consider how engaging, motivating activities can be included in lessons, and how students can be encouraged to apply these skills to real contexts beyond the specific exams.

A further consideration with this model is that it implies that the skills tested in Unit 1 are somehow disjointed, both from each other and from those tested in Units 2, 3 and 4. Students are inclined to think they have 'done credibility', for example, and can now forget about it. Equally, if this model is combined with fully explicit skills teaching, it does not fully allow for the long-term, ongoing development of important skills such as developing reasoning, or the use of thinking and reasoning skills to form judgements and make decisions. This can be remedied by building in possibilities for students to develop reasoning – perhaps by having discussions about current affairs and asking students to support their views in speech or writing; asking students to write arguments to support or counter those in the practice texts you are using; or adapting a mixed explicit/embedded approach rather than fully explicit approach to teaching and practising thinking and reasoning skills. We will discuss how to plan the mixed approach later.

Structure around topics

Another option is to structure the course around topics, blocking topics to weeks of the course.

IGCSE Global Perspectives
Weeks 1-4: Water
Weeks 5-8: Education
Weeks 10-14: Conflict

This approach ensures that students have worked in some of the areas mentioned on the syllabus, but there is a risk that teachers will teach issues and content relating to these topics rather than encouraging students to develop their own thinking and reasoning skills. By focusing on the information rather than the skills, students would be remembering and understanding; low-level skills according to Bloom's Revised Taxonomy (BRT) (see the diagram and discussion of BRT on page 48). The higher-level skills that are listed in the syllabus also need to be planned in.

IGCSE Global Perspectives has two structures that can be used to shape planning within each topic. One or both of these could be used to inform planning of other courses with a significant element of thinking and reasoning skills. These are the Teaching and Learning Process (TLP) and the thinking about Local, National and International issues. Here, we will concentrate on the use of the TLP to plan a Global Perspectives course, and its possible application to mixed explicit/implicit teaching in other qualifications.

The Teaching and Learning Process

The Teaching and Learning Process requires that in each topic, students:

- collect;
- question;
- reflect and plan;
- present/act.

Collection requires students to choose a topic and narrow down a research area or question, then use research skills to collect information.

Questioning requires students to consider the credibility and reliability of sources, examine the knowledge claims they contain (how do they know?), consider the quality of reasoning in the sources, and select and discard sources. It may be that students need to return to the collection stage if they have discarded most of their sources, or if their questioning has led to the need for more information.

Reflection and planning involve a consideration of the values the students have come across and of their own position in relation to these. Students need to consider also the likelihood and plausibility of any suggested consequences, and what these might lead to. At this stage, students should think through possible future scenarios and evaluate their seriousness and likelihood. They need to reflect on the issues and their own opinions regarding them in the light of the evidence they have considered, and should begin to plan either an active project or a presentation.

Presentation requires students to communicate the product of their thinking in a way that is accessible to their peers and that communicates their thinking and reasoning. This might take the form of an active project, such as a series of tee shirts with images representing issues in their chosen subject, together with an evaluative report on the process. Alternatively, it might be a class discussion, written piece of work, poem, video, poster and talk, performed dialogue, or seminar.

Using the Teaching and Learning Process to inform planning

So, let's look at how the Teaching and Learning Process might inform planning.

Weeks 1–4: Family

Aims: Students investigate family and demographic issues around the world. They begin to learn about and apply the skills in the TLP.
Outcome: Students produce a wall display to include images, diagrams, annotated source material and written work in the form of a poster.

Week One

- Teacher provides stimulus material (e.g. Donna material from Chapter 1 (see pages 10 and 18).
- Teacher guides students to think through:
  a) issues to do with family – make a reusable spider diagram of various issues (*collecting and framing ideas so that the research part of the collection process is focused; beginning to reflect*);
  b) issues to do with how we know information, where it comes from, and how we use it to help up make decisions (*questioning, with the beginnings of reflection*).

Week Two

- Students research information in groups about specific aspects of family life around the world, e.g. laws relating to marriage, age of adulthood, or customs. These may have emerged from the discussion in Week One, or could be given to students by the teacher. The framing of the research areas should allow students to make comparisons between national and international norms (*collecting*).
- Teacher-led class discussion concerning the quality of any sources found and the consequences of this discussion (select, discard, keep looking). Some formalisation of criteria for judging sources, such as expertise of author, motives to be untruthful, corroboration between sources. Some discussion of whether enough of the right sort of information has been collected (*questioning*).

- Students work in groups to consider the quality of their remaining sources and information, fill in any gaps in their information, and start planning their display (*questioning and beginning to reflect*).

Week Three

- Teacher-led discussion of the issues raised by the information students have found, the teacher prompting students to express opinions, justify them and take the new evidence into consideration (*reflection*).
- The teacher leads a session giving students a clear framework for their display, detailing the sorts of annotation (e.g. a printed source with annotation such as, 'This information comes from www.mumsnet.com, so it's probably not representative, or as authoritative as statistics from a government agency, but it is first-hand evidence of how people feel about family issues, and it shows the debate'), and the nature of the written work (e.g. an opinion justified with reasons and reference to some of the evidence), reminding students to use images, and eliciting students' ideas.
- Students reflect on the issues, plan, and begin putting together their display. The teacher moves around groups, helping them to work in the right direction, raising questions, joining discussions etc. (*reflection, planning and beginnings of presentation*).

Week Four

- Students work in groups to complete their displays. The teacher moves around the groups, reminding students of the deadline, and encouraging them to use their newly developed skills and not just copy and paste (*reflection and presentation*).
- Displays are put on the wall (*presentation*).
- The teacher gathers feedback from students and reminds them of the skills they have practised (*questioning information, reflecting on it and using it to justify an opinion*), then asks students to write down what they think they can do to improve next time.

Weeks 5–8: Education

Similar process: reliability of sources and information practised, and emphasis in Week Two on identifying different types of reasoning.

Weeks 20–23: Students choose topics in groups
Week One
The teacher helps students to refine a research area and define an outcome (marketing campaign, tee shirt design, student newsletter, song etc.). Students collect information and question it. Teacher walks round groups prompting them to question using the skills they have developed so far during the course, such as considering the reliability of a source, the type of evidence, the type of reasoning.

Week Two
Students reflect on the information and plan how they will achieve their outcome.

Week Three
Students work towards their outcome.

Week Four
Students produce their outcome (*act*) and write an evaluation of the process. An example might be:

> Producing a thirty-minute video to highlight the plight of endangered species was too ambitious for the time available. It didn't help that we forgot to share our files, so when Xavier was ill, none of us could edit the video. But I've learned a lot about time planning and using my thinking skills for a practical project. I hadn't realised they would help so much. Next time I won't work with Xavier, he doesn't do enough.

Groups of students give feedback to other students (e.g. 'We really liked your group's use of humour, it made your video more appealing than doom-and-gloom videos. We think that to improve, you could make a shorter video, and edit it more carefully, because it seemed a bit like you ran out of time at the end.')

This option allows a gradual development of skills in context with slowly increasing student independence. It will still need to be planned and monitored carefully to ensure that teacher and student focus does not drift too far from the thinking and reasoning skills that attract marks in the final assessment. There is a case for the course planner to include materials for some explicit skills teaching to help teachers formalise the skills developed and applied during the TLP.

Applying ideas from the TLP to other qualifications

To what extent, then, can the IGCSE Global Perspectives Teaching and Learning Process be used in other qualifications to help contextualise the skills? There are a number of ways this could be done. Let's look again at OCR GCE AS Critical Thinking and map the skills in the specification to the TLP.

Collect: Students do not have to collect information for this assessment. All materials are provided in the examination. Does this mean that there is no role for collecting information and applying skills to that information during the teaching process?

Question: Consider the credibility and reliability of evidence/source material (Unit 1). Identify different types of reasoning and elements of that reasoning (Units 1 and 2, mostly 1). Evaluate the use of evidence to support a claim (Unit 2). Evaluate the quality of reasoning (Units 1 and 2, mostly 2).

Reflect: Consider values (Principles in Unit 2). Consider the plausibility and likelihood of consequences (Plausibility and likelihood in Unit 1, evaluating hypothetical reasoning in Unit 2). Think about issues (Unit 2, developing reasoning – better students reflect on the issue as well as the structure of the argument). Plan (Unit 2, developing reasoning – better students plan). Make judgements (Unit 1, students must make a judgement about an issue; Unit 2, students must come to a conclusion when they develop reasoning).

Present: In this examination, presenting comes in the form of answering a variety of examination questions. Does this mean that this is the only way students should present during the course? Could students develop skills of questioning, reflecting and planning through other forms of presentation?

This mapping indicates that it would be possible to apply the teaching and learning process to preparing candidates for a fully examined qualification such as OCR's GCE AS Critical Thinking. Despite the differences in examination style and level of skill (an AS examination, of course, is designed to test the skills at a higher level than an IGCSE), the qualifications have a similar core of skills. There are a number of options.

Option A

Block lessons by skill, but treat each as a mini version of the TLP. Although the focus would be on a specific skill, this would be developed in the context of a lesson in which students discussed issues and developed reasoning as well. This would have the additional benefit of bringing the judgement formation process into every lesson, and making it clear to students that it should follow from the processes of considering evidence and reasoning.

Lesson One might look like this:

- Teacher displays the question, 'What do you think Donna should do?'
- Students question the source material (see pages 10 and 16), learning to identify arguments and differentiate from other kinds of reasoning.
- Students reflect on the different kinds of reasoning, and how seriously they should be taken. Students reflect on the issue.
- Students present and justify their opinions (by writing an argument).

Lesson Two might look like this:

- Materials: series of short arguments on issues relating to giving aid to poor countries.
- Teacher displays the question: 'Should we give aid to poor countries?'
- Brief class discussion, drawing out issues relating to who 'we' are, what 'aid' is and what 'poor countries' are. (This is a form of *collection*, setting a starting point and clarifying terms.)
- Teacher elicits from students the definition of an argument from Lesson One. Talks about identifying reasons and conclusion. The teacher shows students how to use colours to highlight different argument elements by taking a simple argument and highlighting the reasons blue and the conclusion red. The teacher rearranges the argument to show reasons first and conclusion last with 'therefore' written in a third colour.
- Students work in groups to identify reasons and conclusion, using different colours (*questioning*).
- Game to reinforce learning (see Chapters 4 and 5 for games ideas).
- Teacher asks whether students have changed their minds in the light of new ideas and evidence. Students prepare short arguments in groups (*reflecting and taking questioned evidence into consideration*), then open debate between groups (*presenting*).

Option B

Three four-week topics or four three-week topics plus two weeks of focused Unit 1 exam practice, Unit 1 taken in January. Map skills to be covered for exam in each topic, and mix embedded learning with explicit learning. Include opportunities for revisiting and reinforcing skills.

Option C

Both units of AS examination to be taken in May. Divide the year into three- or four-week topics and map the examination skills onto the topics, allowing for slow, gradual progress and reinforcing skills.

The critical path

Pre-U Global Perspectives and Independent Research Report has its own teaching and learning process, called the Critical Path. Its stages are:

- *Deconstruction*: setting a research question, clarifying terms, analysing and evaluating arguments.
- *Reconstruction*: setting a single argument in its broader (generally global) context, beginning to understand different perspectives on an issue, considering the relative strength of the evidence base for different views and perspectives.
- *Reflection*: thinking deeply about issues in the light of work done during deconstruction and reconstruction; going beyond one's own perspective.
- *Presentation*: presentation is assessed by written examination, essay (in the form of a literature review) and audio presentation making a case (and using visual aids). Presentations in teaching can take many forms. Students must engage with at least two perspectives.

This is a more advanced version of the IGCSE TLP, with its sights set firmly on preparing candidates for university. It focuses more on reconstructing a whole context and engaging sympathetically and intellectually with different perspectives than the IGCSE Global Perspectives Teaching and Learning Process. Again, it can be adapted for use in other qualifications – and to include ideas from other qualifications.

Discussion
Which of the ideas here can you use to inform your course planning? Which approaches seem most suitable for you, your school, your colleagues, your students and the qualification you are working with? How can you adapt the ideas to suit your own needs? Revisit your

ideas from the first discussion in this chapter and see to what extent they have developed. Use your log book to record and chase your ideas.

Planning visual material

One final consideration in this section about how to prepare students for the examination relates to visual learning materials. Students can find it very helpful to have their learning reinforced by visual displays in the classroom. These aids might be key terms and definitions, questions, diagrams of argument structure, student work showing evidence of thinking skills, posters ... If you have a classroom or part of a classroom where this kind of work can be displayed, it is helpful to do so. This means planning time for students to produce the work. It doesn't need to be a long time, and can follow naturally from some of the presentation work that students do. This kind of display can also be useful in selling the course to new students.

 Use your log book to make notes on where in your course it would be helpful/possible to allocate time for display work.

Further Questions

By now you have the tools to arrange or rearrange your course, to try new approaches, reflect on them and amend or discard them as appropriate. There are, however, a number of other considerations, including the following.

- Who is teaching? What are their abilities and needs?
- Who is learning? What are their abilities and needs?
- How much time is available?
- What resources do we have/need?
- Is there anything in the specific nature of my school or college that will affect my planning?

Who is teaching? What are their abilities and needs?

If you are the subject coordinator, the number, nature and experience of the staff teaching your course will have an effect on your planning. If you are lucky you will have a team of volunteers who are naturally inclined to think and reason critically, and who have some experience of the teaching and learning styles involved in developing thinking and reasoning skills. In this case, you can plan fairly loosely, relying on your colleagues to find and share materials, focus on the appropriate skills and respond to particular student needs.

If you are less lucky – and you will not be alone – you may have a resentful group of teachers who have been told that they must teach your subject (possibly to fill gaps in their timetables). They may lack the inclination to think and reason critically or turn their thinking skills against the nearest figure with any authority (you). This is an uncomfortable position for you to be in, but it is worth remembering that, in most cases, these staff are probably feeling undervalued and put upon. If you can listen to them, value their contribution and support them in areas where they have difficulties, they can become excellent thinking teachers who enjoy their new subject. You may have to plan more tightly, though, providing more support and resources.

Typically, staff teaching subjects with a significant element of thinking and reasoning skills come from a variety of subject backgrounds. You may have scientists or artists in your team who have experience with managing groups of students engaged in practical work. You may have musicians experienced in skill building and mixed ability teaching requiring advanced differentiation. You may have language teachers with experience of developing language skills and knowing plenty of games for internalising structures. This is a hugely rich resource for you to rely on.

Discussion

What skills do your staff have? How can you find out? How can you encourage staff to share ideas? Could you have a half-day where everyone shares their best lesson ideas from their main subjects and then works in teams to adapt to the new subject?

Is there anyone who could help to support the less confident members of the team? Could someone produce and share materials, or could each member of the team produce materials for a part of the course? What are the team's training needs? Do you have enough staff to invite an expert from the exam board to join you – or can you band together with some other schools to arrange for this training? Can you observe each other's lessons? If you are all from different subject areas you may well have good ideas to share. Have you visited exam board web-based support forums?

Who is Learning? What are Their Abilities and Needs?

It goes without saying that the varying needs of the students in your school or college will affect your planning.

More able students often respond better to stimulus materials that challenge their abilities to form beliefs, make judgements and take decisions than to materials that seem to be overly simple in terms of the content. The challenge for the course planner is to provide materials that seem sufficiently challenging in terms of the issues involved, without being so challenging that students neglect to concentrate on the mechanics of the thinking itself. Planning for thinking about thinking (metacognition) at a high level is key here.

If your cohort is predominantly less able, you will need more time and perhaps also to plan for a greater breakdown of skills and more repetition of the basics. Materials will need to be interesting and accessible, but gradually increase in difficulty to prepare students for the level of difficulty required by assessment. These students may also benefit from vocabulary, comprehension and memory exercises, which language teachers can help you to adapt for the purposes of the thinking qualification. Most of all, these students will need the time, support and opportunity to realise that they can think.

Differentiation

If you have a mixed ability group, the challenge for the thinking course planner will be to organise work such that all students are always pushed to think a little more deeply, both about content and about the thinking itself. Able students need to have intellectually challenging activities whilst less able students need to be pushed beyond their own boundaries. Open-ended discussions about questions to which there is no answer can help with this. Students of all abilities need to practise the skills, both explicitly and embedded in a context. Understanding a metacognitive concept quickly does not entail the ability to remember, use or apply that concept.

Let's look again at Donna's decision to leave school and get married (see pages 10–18). The stimulus here is simple and accessible, so the planner needs to find ways to build in a challenge for the more able. Very able students may find the 'answer' obvious – clearly Donna should stay at school. Perhaps they need to be challenged to get beyond their own perspective and begin to understand Donna's perspective. Another challenge in this situation is to go beyond the content and start thinking about what we can know, how we can know it, and what knowledge is anyway. Is certainty the same as knowledge? Why? Another challenge might be to ask the most able students to think about the different roles that values, emotions and evidence have in decision making. Is it more important to know what Donna's job prospects might be or that she values a loving family life more highly than career success?

We can see, then, that planning for differentiation might mean giving different groups of students different questions to think about, based on the same stimulus material.

Discussion
What sort of students do you have? Look back at the different suggestions for structuring the course, and consider them with differentiation in mind. Which approaches will best allow teachers to support students at their own ability level (without working themselves too hard)? If you already have resources, how much adaptation do you think they need, in the light of last year's experience and the thinking you have done in this chapter? What ideas do the teachers in your team have for keeping all students challenged and motivated?

How Much Time is Available?

Telling students about thinking skills does not take very much time. Assisting students to develop and apply their own thinking skills independently in a variety of contexts can take rather longer. Your ability to plan for students to practise their thinking and reasoning skills will be limited by the time you have available.

What Resources Do We Have/Need?

The thinking course planner – like any other course planner – will need to work round available resources. If a qualification-specific textbook is available, it should be planned in to the course. Endorsed textbooks written by examiners often include material and exam tips that are very helpful when preparing for a specific course. There are other books available, many (though not all) of which are excellent. Past exam papers, mark schemes and examiners' reports are also useful, and can be planned into the course. Towards the end of the course it is highly beneficial for students to mark each other's work and really engage with what the examiner is looking for in an answer.

Other resources include, but are not limited to: newspaper articles, online materials, numerical evidence, reports, poems, stories, letters to newspapers, blogs, comments on newspaper websites, charity websites, and television and radio programmes, especially those where evidence is used, such as documentaries, or where politicians and other leading national figures discuss important and topical issues. Resources for subjects prioritising the development of thinking skills are readily available, and are cheap if you are happy to adapt them yourself. See Chapter 5 for a discussion on adapting resources for your own needs.

Is There Anything in the Specific Nature of My School that Will Affect my Planning?

There are sometimes other, school-specific issues that will affect planning. Some schools use thinking subjects to replace or enhance their delivery of religious education or citizenship, for example. In this case it will be necessary to map areas where RE or citizenship issues can be considered. In other schools the curriculum planners may map the skills and content against the rest of the curriculum. This would both reduce the amount of time needed for specific teaching of the thinking subject and enhance embedded skills practice throughout the curriculum.

Discussion
What issues in your school will affect your planning of the thinking course?

4   Planning a Lesson

Most thinking teachers are experienced at planning lessons in their main subjects, and will be able to transfer their skills to planning thinking lessons. There are, however, a number of differences between teaching traditional, content-based subjects, and teaching that prioritises the development of thinking and reasoning skills. These differences will affect lesson planning decisions; in particular:

- The need to remember and understand[6] specific information can dominate traditional subject teaching, and although students are expected to engage in historical, scientific or ethical thinking, thinking skills are generally not made explicit in traditional subject teaching.
- Teaching that prioritises the development of thinking and reasoning skills can happen within the framework of traditional subject or content teaching, but normally also involves some element of explicit skills teaching. This explicit element of the teaching enables students to think about thinking, and to use this thinking to improve their own thinking and reasoning.

We will discuss the process of planning a thinking lesson, considering ideas for games and activities.

Aims, Objectives and Means

When planning a lesson, the thinking teacher needs to consider the following questions:

- What are the broad aims I am trying to meet?
- What are the more specific objectives I am trying to meet?
- What are the means I am going to use to achieve these aims and objectives?

Aims

The broad aims of a thinking course are likely to include (but not normally be limited to):

- enabling students to think for themselves;
- enabling students to think about their thinking and thus improve it;
- preparing students to cope with the vast quantities of information available to them;
- preparing students to cope with the diversity of people and perspectives they are likely to encounter;
- giving students the tools to form judgements and make decisions;
- giving students the tools to develop reasoning which takes critical evaluation of evidence and other views into consideration.

Some courses also aim to develop students' understanding of issues of importance in the world today, or to develop the ability to understand issues from, for example, an ethical or cultural perspective. However, specific issues or content are not normally prescribed for these courses, and there are generally few, if any, marks available in assessed work for remembering and understanding information and issues. The issues are more normally a vehicle for developing thinking and reasoning skills than an end in themselves. It is therefore not normal for the aim(s) of a thinking lesson to refer to content, subject matter or issues.

If you are teaching thinking and reasoning skills through the traditional curriculum, you may have parallel aims relating to both skills and content. This will require very careful planning, and constant awareness of the dual aims (see Chapter 7).

Remember to check the Aims section of the current syllabus or specification for the qualification you are working with. These can be very helpful in setting the specific skills listed into their broader context.

Objectives

The objectives in a thinking lesson are more specific than the general aims. They are the smaller steps into which the broader aims can be broken down in order to make them gradually achievable. The objectives of a thinking lesson might include one or more of the following (although they are certainly not limited to these):

- students learn how to evaluate the reliability of a source of information;

- students practise evaluating the reliability of source information;
- students apply their ability to evaluate the reliability of source information in the context of a research project;
- students learn to recognise major flaws in reasoning;
- students learn to evaluate the effect and importance of major flaws in reasoning;
- students practise recognising and evaluating flaws in reasoning;
- students apply their ability to recognise and evaluate flawed reasoning in the context of a research project.

When setting objectives for a lesson, the thinking teacher needs to consider how each objective relates to the overall aims of the course and helps students to achieve these broader aims. Objectives are likely to be closely related to the skills in the specification or syllabus.

Objectives in explicit skills teaching

If you are teaching skills explicitly (see Chapter 2 for a discussion of explicit and embedded skills teaching), one by one, then it is likely that each of your lessons will have two or perhaps three objectives relating to a single skill, as follows.

Lesson One: Identifying Arguments
Aim: Analyse reasoning (in order to judge usefulness in research context).
Objective 1: Learn to identify arguments as written or spoken attempts to persuade an audience to accept a conclusion on the basis of one or more (rational) reasons (as opposed to emotional persuasion or threats of violence).
Objective 2: Learn to discriminate between arguments and other kinds of writing such as report, opinion, rant, explanation.
Objective 3: Practise the skills outlined in Objectives 1 and 2.

Lesson Two: Identifying Conclusions and Reasons
Aim: Analyse reasoning (in order to judge usefulness in research context).
Objective 1: Learn to recognise what you are being persuaded to accept (identify conclusion).
Objective 2: Learn to recognise on what grounds you are being persuaded to accept a conclusion (identify reasons).
Objective 3: Practise the skills outlined in Objectives 1 and 2.

Remember always to refer to the current syllabus or specification you are working with to ensure you are covering precisely the right skills. Qualifications differ concerning when to introduce the distinction between argument and explanation, for example. It is also useful to be guided by a qualification-specific textbook and by past examination papers.

Objectives in embedded skills teaching

If you are teaching skills embedded in a context, you are likely to have two, three or perhaps four objectives for every lesson, generally relating to different skills. These objectives will recur frequently, but you may give one of them a higher importance in a particular lesson. Let's consider extracts from a plan for a four-week project on conflict, occurring towards the end of the first year of teaching. There are three lessons a week, and most skills have already been introduced and practised to some extent.

Overall aims for the four-week project:

- To develop students' ability to take other perspectives seriously, and to form judgements in challenging circumstances.
- To support students in independent work that takes them out of their comfort zone.

Overall objectives:

- To practise and apply the skill of finding, evaluating the quality and reliability of source material.
- To practise and apply the skill of selecting and making evaluative use of source material.
- To use first person narrative, film and poetry to help students to engage with perspectives other than their own.
- To reflect on the issues such that students make informed judgements, making critical use of and following from their evaluation and consideration of source material.

Outcome of project: presentation (various formats to be negotiated with students).

Lesson One:
Objective 1: students are confronted with and begin to engage with a perspective that will challenge them.
Objective 2: students consider some of the kinds and strength of reasoning used to support the challenging perspective.

Objective 3: students consider the unstated aspects of the challenging perspective.

Objective 4: students begin to reflect on issues raised by the challenging perspective and articulate this reflection.

Lesson Four:

Objective 1: students evaluate the source materials they have found during research (in Lessons Two and Three) in terms of their reliability, strength and usefulness.

Objective 2: students identify gaps in their information/knowledge/understanding that need to be filled by further research.

Objective 3: students continue to reflect on their relationship to the challenging perspective.

Objective 4: students continue to plan their presentation.

Lesson Nine

Objective 1: Students present.

Objective 2: Students evaluate each other's work in a formative way, based on how they have represented, evaluated and responded to the challenging perspective.

These extracts indicate how lesson objectives develop over a four-week project, and how they are revisited, practised and applied in context. We can also see that the objectives all relate to the skills being developed in the context of conflict, rather than to the specific knowledge about conflict that students are to gain.

Conflict could relate to family conflict, friendship conflict, divorce, terrorism, war ... Materials could relate to divorce, America's 'War on terror', local conflicts in your part of the world, border problems between India and China or India and Pakistan, violence in Northern Ireland ...

Do I have to plan lessons like this?

Your lesson planning does not always have to happen in this linear fashion. Sometimes you will have an inspiration for an activity, and only later realise how it can help you achieve your aims and objectives. At other times you will come across a newspaper article, poem, report on the radio, or television programme, and think, 'I can use that', and then work out how it can fit into your overall aims.

What matters is not the order in which you think through things, but the *process* of thinking through how your activities and specific lessons relate to your overall goals as part of your reflective practice. By articulating and thinking through the thinking you use when planning and evaluating lessons you can improve your teaching.

One of the delights of thinking courses is that teachers and students can follow their interests rather than a fixed curriculum. Problems occur when teachers lose sight of the aims and objectives of the course. In thinking subjects, the most common problem is focusing on content rather than skills, closely followed by focusing on the mechanics of skills isolated from their purpose and the overall aims of the course.

Discussion
How do you plan lessons in your main subject? Which of these skills can you transfer to planning thinking lessons? Do you like to start from broad goals or specific activities? Do you like to integrate a number of skills or work on one thing at a time? Do your students think in the same way as you? Use your log book to think through these issues.

Means

The means used to achieve the aims and objectives of a lesson are the specific activities. As discussed above, you may think of an activity before you have fully articulated your objectives, but it is of fundamental importance to the success of your teaching that the activities in your lesson help students to achieve the aims and objectives. When you think of an activity, you should always ask yourself:

- How can this activity help students achieve the aims of the course?
- How will this activity help students to achieve the objectives of this lesson?

You may find that you have to postpone some exciting activities until later in the course, adapt them, or even discard them if you realise that they are not helping students to meet these aims and objectives.

What sort of activities can meet thinking objectives?

Almost any activity can help to meet thinking objectives in one way or another, so long as there is a focus on developing thinking and reasoning skills rather than, say, acquiring knowledge. The thinking teacher's staple activities include the following.

Debate and discussion

Debate and discussion are a very good way of encouraging students to reflect, take evidence and alternative perspectives into consideration, and learn respectful ways to respond to others' views without simply dismissing them. Students can also evaluate their own and each other's reasoning in the context of a debate or discussion. Students develop and use these skills in the context of an issue that motivates them, and can therefore see the point. The teacher needs to ensure that the students become aware of the thinking they are doing as well as the issue they are thinking about.

Games and competitions

Games and competitions can, carefully managed, motivate students to practise skills explicitly with an enthusiasm they never build up for straight skills practice. Games can be excellent for internalising thinking structures, encouraging students to repeat a skill far more often than they would without the game. It is often worth playing team rather than individual games, so that no single person either wins or loses. Alternatively, play games where winning or losing is more or less unrelated to the skills being used.

Games of chance can be adapted to incorporate thinking and reasoning skills practice. The children's board game, Snakes and Ladders, for example, can easily be adapted. Dice are rolled to determine how many steps can be taken towards the goal. If a player finishes at the bottom of a ladder, they may ascend it. In the skills-based variant, students must answer a skills-based question before ascending a ladder or descending a snake. If they get the answer right then they may ascend the ladder, or avoid having to descend the snake, and vice versa if they get the answer wrong. Students' ability to answer the questions is combined with the chance rolls of the dice, so students who lose do not need to feel disheartened about their skills. The questions used could be made up by the teacher on the spot, be prepared in advance by the teacher or students, or be past exam questions turned into games cards. The game could focus on one particular skill, such as identifying unstated assumptions or evaluating flawed reasoning, or be used to test students' ability in a range of different skills.

Grandmother's footsteps is another game that can be adapted. In the children's game, one person stands facing the wall at one end of the room, whilst others try to creep up. Occasionally, the person facing the wall turns round. If they see anyone moving, that person goes back to the beginning. The player who touches the person by the wall wins. In the skills-based variant, anyone who is seen to move must answer a question.

If they get the answer correct, they stay where they are, but if they get it wrong, they must return to the beginning.

Articulate™ can be used in its original form sometimes. Players work in teams to describe people, places, actions, concepts or things without using the words given on the card. This is an excellent game for improving students' articulacy, their ability to think around a subject and under time pressure, and their general knowledge, all of which help in the pressure of a timed written examination testing thinking and reasoning skills. It can also be adapted to include key terms from the language of reasoning such as 'assumption' or 'conclusion' or 'counter-argument', or any other terms that seem appropriate.

Other board games can be adapted for use in the thinking classroom, as can popular television quiz shows. In 'Who Wants to be a Thinker?' multiple choice questions can be practised, with one student at the front answering questions, the rest of the class constantly paying attention in case the 'contestant' opts to ask the audience or 'phone' a friend.

Students enjoy preparing games. They can be very inventive and, even at 18, enjoy playing games of their own devising. The task of preparing such games is probably even better skills practice than playing them. Only two rules are necessary:

- the game must focus on skills rather than knowledge;
- students must have the game fully prepared by the deadline, or they will do a practice examination paper instead.

Kinaesthetic activities

Activities that require students to move around can be very helpful. Moving helps us to think better, changes our perspective on what is happening, and gives us a body memory. Some students learn significantly better when they can move parts of an argument around as sheets of coloured, laminated paper than when the argument elements are only ideas.

One useful form of kinaesthetic activity involves giving each student a card with a part of an argument printed on it. Students have to move around the room finding other students with parts of the same argument, and then reassemble it. There are many variants of this sort of 'cut up and find your partners' activity.

Another useful form of kinaesthetic activity is asking students to move to different parts of the room depending on their opinions on an issue. The simplest form of this is, 'agree' on one side of the room, 'disagree' on the other side, and 'don't know' in the middle. The teacher then asks for students to justify their opinion. Students move around as their opinion changes during the discussion. This activity can give students the confidence to voice their opinions more than if they are sitting in their seats.

One variant of this activity involves the teacher introducing (surprising) new evidence, and asking students how this evidence affects their opinions. This focuses on the skills of assessing the impact of new evidence and adapting our judgements accordingly. Another variant can involve clarifying the language and assumptions used by people who hold different views. For example, people in favour of abortion tend to talk of 'terminating cell clusters'; those against it, of 'killing children'. This can lead to an interesting lesson on the importance of unstated parts of an argument, concepts that underlie language use, and how these affect the strength of an argument and the judgements we make on that argument's basis.

Research projects

Research projects lie at the heart of embedded skills teaching, and can be used in predominantly explicit skills teaching as a means of practising and applying thinking and reasoning skills. We will discuss how to organise research projects in more detail below (see page 82).

Display work

Preparing visual materials for the classroom and corridors can help students to improve their thinking and reasoning skills and also to understand and internalise them. The visual and kinaesthetic activities of arranging display work can in themselves aid learning. In addition, the activity of thinking through how an abstraction such as an argument or an issue can be represented visually can really help students to understand the sorts of thinking they are doing and the focus on skills rather than content. Furthermore, display work can reinforce learning just by being visible to students.

Display work can be highly sophisticated, allowing students to use their generally highly advanced Information and Communication Technology (ICT) skills in real contexts. Scribbling on sugar paper is a useful way of developing ideas, but is rarely appropriate for a finished product. IGCSE Global Perspectives, for example, allows candidates to produce visual material as part of the Portfolio assessment, and the outcome of the Project might be a pamphlet, brochure, advert or student/community newsletter. Pre-U Global Perspectives requires a presentation in which candidates talk using a visual aid, which could be a poster, for example. Students need to use technology in appropriate ways in the assessment. Practice for any of these allows display work to be integrated naturally into your planning and teaching. If you are teaching a fully examined qualification, it may still be appropriate to use some of these ideas as part of your practice.

Display work can grow out of almost any other activities, but the thinking teacher needs to plan materials, access to ICT, deadlines, support for students and most importantly, the framework within which students will be operating. Students will require very clear guidance on what they are displaying and how to do so. The following are some, but by no means all, of the types of display that might be integrated into thinking lessons.

Students might produce a photograph display relating to a topic they have studied, with written work explaining the thinking processes. For example, students in Argentina might correspond by email or Skype with students in the UK in order to compare and evaluate the effects of immigration on the two countries. They could take photographs representing some of the issues in their own country, and share these, along with their ideas, with students in the other country. In order to fully engage with the perspectives of the people in the photographs, students might research why people migrate, why they cling to their language and culture and/or why people are made uneasy by immigrants. The display would include photographs from both countries, as well as written work – probably a reasoned case supporting a viewpoint.

Another form of display work that can be effective is cutting up arguments to show the structure. Reasons can be backed on blue paper, for example, the main conclusion on red, evidence and examples on yellow, intermediate conclusions on green, and counter-arguments on pink. These parts of the argument can then be arranged to show its logical structure, with the conclusion at the bottom.[7] The arguments used might come from newspapers, magazines or internet sources, or be the students' own arguments. It is useful for students to understand how their individual reasoning works, but structure should only ever be a tool to serve the purpose of answering a question with strong reasoning, and never an end in itself.

Students might produce a display on the theme of 'thinking' in which they visualise the abstract concepts they have been dealing with. Some might produce flow diagrams to represent thinking processes, others annotate a project or piece of work they have done to show the thinking, others again write a poem, song or dialogue, and still others try to represent thinking as a painting, collage or sculpture. It might be possible to collaborate with the art, technology, ICT and/or music departments. Alternatively, an expanded version might be the sort of project that could be used for an Extended Project.

Questioning

One of the main activities in a thinking lesson is questioning, as discussed in Chapter 2 (see pages 47–51). To begin with, you may find it helpful to prepare a number of questions in advance to provoke thought. You could use the discussion in Chapter 2 and Bloom's Revised Taxonomy (BRT) to help you. It may be useful to include a diagram of BRT on the wall of your classroom, to help students think through how different questions call for different skills.

Worksheets

There is, of course, a place for worksheets in the thinking classroom, although if you are not careful they can be overused. Again, think about the sort of questions you are using on them. Do they relate to skills or content? Will they help students to achieve the aims and objectives of your lesson? The danger with worksheets is that they can become a time filler, activities done for the sake of it, rather than because they are valuable. Beware also of 'writing frames' or formulae that will limit rather than improve your candidates' thinking. There are of course structures of thinking and language that it is helpful for candidates to internalise. But adhering rigidly to a structure without regard to the context is not thinking.

Exam practice

The question with exam practice is not whether to use it, but how much to do so. It is, indeed, vital that students are familiar with exam papers and mark schemes, and very useful if they have experience of peer marking so that they can understand how the examiner is thinking. On the other hand, an overdose of exam practice is both dull and stressful and is, furthermore, more likely to lead to students being able to answer exam questions than truly think independently. The thinking teacher therefore needs to include many forms of skills practice, and judge when to introduce exam papers. The activities we have discussed, and many that you can think of yourself, will help students to practise and develop exam skills without causing unnecessary pressure.

Discussion
What games and activities do you use in your main subjects? How can they be adapted to focus on thinking and reasoning skills? What other ideas can you think of? Can you find time to share ideas with colleagues? When you try a new idea, write your thoughts about it in your log book. What worked? Why? What didn't work as well? Why? How could you tweak what you did to improve the lesson?

Judging the Success of a Lesson

It can be difficult to judge the success of a lesson, partly because you are so involved in it that you do not have an objective stance. You may have been so preoccupied with the two students who did not understand or didn't want to participate that you underestimated the value of the 28 students who worked independently and productively. Alternatively, you may have been so disconcerted by the lesson not going to plan that you downplay the value of the direction the lesson actually took.

 People tend to over-emphasise the negative parts of their experience at the expense of the positive. Use your log book to write down how you feel about lessons, and remember to focus on the positive. So the lesson didn't go as planned? What did happen, and what was good about it? Perhaps your students had a deep discussion about the ethics of a recent conflict or terror attack? Which skills did they use? Were their needs more important than the lesson you'd planned, and did you meet these needs?

You could use the following questions to help you judge the success of your lessons.

- Did the lesson meet the objectives?
- Did students go some way towards meeting the aims of the course?
- Did students think independently?
- Did students leave the room still discussing the issue?

If the answer to any of these questions is 'yes' then your lesson has been successful. The key is to achieve the right balance of 'yeses'. If your students regularly think but the lesson rarely meets the objectives, you might find it helpful to consider your approach to ensure that students pass the exam as well as thinking. If your lessons generally meet specific objectives, but you rarely have the impression students are thinking, then it may be time to rework your approach to ensure that students develop their ability to think deeply in context as well as passing the exam.

Another useful self-check question is:

- Who talked more, students or teacher?

If the students talked more than the teacher, there is a strong chance they were thinking, providing they were talking about relevant issues and not their weekend plans. If the students are discussing issues, arguing with each other, making suggestions and asking questions, they are likely to be developing thinking and reasoning skills. They are also likely to be fairly independent and taking control of their own learning. If the teacher talks more than the students on a regular basis, the teacher is probably working too hard and taking too much control.

Organising Activities

When you are planning thinking lessons, it is important to consider how you will organise activities as well as what the activities will be. Because the emphasis is on students practising skills and gaining independence rather than on the teacher transmitting knowledge to students, the teacher's role can be very different in the thinking classroom from the traditional classroom. See Chapter 2 for a discussion of the different roles the thinking teacher might have (see pages 43–51). You could ask yourself questions such as the following to help yourself think through the issues.

- What does the teacher do?
- Where does the teacher stand?
- When does the teacher intervene and when remain silent?
- How does the teacher intervene?

There are no fixed, 'right' answers to these questions. Use your log book to help you think through various possible answers. Add to your thoughts as you read through this section.

What does the teacher do?

What the teacher does should depend on what the teacher wants the students to do. If students are engaged in skills practice or independent research, the teacher is likely to walk round the room questioning students, pushing them to think more deeply, reminding them to use and apply the skills they have learned. If students are engaged in a kinaesthetic activity, the teacher may need to pay particular attention to health and safety issues. At other times, they may instruct the class from the front.

Creating a framework

One of the main things that the teacher does is set up activities within a framework, so that students have a clear understanding of what they are aiming to achieve and how they are supposed to achieve this. There is a balance to be found between over- and under-organising. Let's look at three ways of setting up a research project. All three lessons occur towards the end of the first year of a two-year Level 3 qualification. Students are around 17.

Example A

> **Teacher:** *Right, listen. You're going to do a research project on emergency aid following natural disasters. Use the computers. You've got three weeks. Off you go.*

This teacher has under-organised: the students in this class are likely to feel lost and abandoned. They do know the general topic and time frame, but are unlikely to have a clear idea of what the outcome of their project should be. They are likely to collect some information, but not really know what to do with it. What outcome are they producing? What is the research question? How will they present their information? Should they argue, report, explain?

Example B

> **Teacher:** *We're going to do a research project. The question is, 'To what extent is emergency aid effective in the aftermath of natural disasters?'*

[Displays and talks through handout]

> *Step 1:* Use the following websites: www.xyz.org; www.abc.com; www.pqr.ca.
> *Step 2:* Use this outline to record the major issues [show basic spider diagram].
> *Step 3:* Assess the credibility of the sources as follows: 'The credibility of www.xyz.org is very high because it is a government-run agency, which means that it is unlikely to lie.'
> *Step 4:* Make two lists under the headings, 'effective' and 'ineffective'.
> *Step 5:* Write an essay using the following writing frame ...

Although well-meaning, this teacher has over-organised:

- There is very little thinking left for students to do. Although none of these steps is entirely without its place, the cumulative effect of this list is to disempower students. Their role has become mere gap filling, adding information to the structure of someone else's thinking. However weak students are, they deserve to be given the opportunity to structure their own thinking.

- The teacher has told students which resources to use. In what way, then, is this a research project? Researching resources is not about following a web link; it is about trawling through material until appropriate material is found. With younger students or very weak students it may be appropriate to narrow the research area down from 'the internet', but the students need to play an increasing role in helping to restrict the search field.

- The teacher has limited the way students think about the reliability and usefulness of sources to a single formula which allows little room for subtlety. Furthermore, there seems to be little point in assessing the credibility of sources when these have been specifically chosen. The point of assessing reliability and credibility is to decide whether or not to use a particular source of information at all.

- The teacher has determined what shape students' preliminary thinking should take by determining not only that they should use one particular kind of diagram, but by providing the shape of that diagram. What if the student has a different mental picture of the relationships between the issues? There are many different ways of visualising thinking and the relationships between issues, and the aim of a thinking course is that students should be able to develop their own.

- The teacher has encouraged candidates to think about the issue as a dichotomy between effective and ineffective, rather than as a sliding scale of effectiveness. Although there is a role for considering the evidence base for an argument and counter-argument, or for different perspectives, framing the discussion in this way as 'for' and 'against' limits the subtlety of understanding that students are likely to use.

- As for a writing frame for 17-year-olds halfway through a thinking course... if you picture the author with steam hissing from her ears, and flames from her nostrils, you are close to the truth. There is a fundamental difference between supporting students to think in a structured way and imposing a specific structure to limit their thinking.

Example C

Teacher: *We're going to start work on a mini-research project today. We'll be doing three of these by the end of term, and hopefully you'll get some ideas for your Independent Study next year. This study is in groups, the next will be in pairs, and the third will be individual work. We've got one group working in the area of emergency aid, one considering the ethics of food aid, one looking at child-sponsorship programmes and one looking at payment for charity chief executives. Okay, look at this.*

[Displays and talks]

Outcome: group presentation, spoken with visual aids – poster, photographs and captions, pamphlet, or other visual of your choice. Max talking time ten minutes. You must present a reasoned case, not just give facts. You must consider and argue against (refute) an alternative perspective or counter-argument.
Time limit: You've got three weeks. What else do you need?
Student A: *A research question?*
Teacher: *Yes. What are the characteristics of a good research question?*
Student B: *You can argue about it. That means, there's a real debate, and it's something that requires evaluative argument, not just explanation or fact giving.*
Student C: *You can answer it in the time or word limit.*
Student D: *There are suitable resources available.*
Student E: *It's interesting.*
Teacher: *Yes, that's a really important one. What's the point of choosing a research question you don't care about the answer to? D, you mentioned resources. What do you mean by 'suitable'?*
Student D: *Reliable, written by people who know what they're talking about, using strong arguments, recent, relevant, corroborated – not just a lone person with strange ideas.*
Teacher: *So, let's see if you can sort out your research questions and start researching by the end of today. Remember that your question must meet the characteristics you just told me about.*

[Teacher walks round groups, asking them to explain their thinking, questioning, checking that students are developing research questions which will enable them to meet the criteria. For example: 'Do you really think you can do all that in three weeks? You're asking an awful lot of yourself.' 'The general area is interesting, but where is the debate? What's the alternative perspective? ... Oh, yes, now I see. I hadn't thought of that.' 'I haven't got a clear idea of your direction. Can you explain it to me?' 'Do you think people really think that? Are you setting up a bit of a straw person, just to knock it down? Is that quite fair?']

This teacher is not perfect, and has not come up with the only 'right' answer to setting up a research project. But there are many strengths to this form of setting the framework for a research project.

- The students have been given a context for the research project, and should understand the overall aim of helping them to prepare for an independent study.
- The students have a clear outcome to help them structure and plan their research and thinking.
- The students and teacher have negotiated the framework to some extent. This gives students some control and ownership of their work, but the teacher is still clearly in control of the learning environment.
- The teacher has asked the students to remind each other of the skills they need to apply to this project in the early stages. It is clear that students are familiar with these skills and have had practice in applying them. This is a strong platform for the teacher to push them to apply the skills with more subtlety and finesse.
- The teacher is helping the students to frame the research area and structure their own thinking.
- The students are developing independence.

Discussion
What strategies do you use when you set up activities? How do you frame a task for students? Who does the work? Can you think of any other ideas for setting up activities? What if students don't know what they are doing? How can you improve what you are doing? How can you make the framework clearer?

Where does the teacher stand?

Where the teacher stands (or sits) depends on what is happening in the classroom. Sometimes it will be appropriate to stand at the front of the class, sometimes at the back; sometimes the teacher should sit with one group of students, or set up a desk in a quiet corner to have meetings with individuals. What happens when you move away from the front of the classroom?

Intervening

There are a number of different ways in which a teacher can intervene during a thinking lesson including:

- ask a question;
- model a strong answer;
- suggest a counter-argument;
- make a correction;
- make a statement.

All of these have a place, although the first three tend to be more positive and lead to more student thinking. Students will sometimes get the wrong answer, but they can be helped to correct themselves rather than being told the right one. Let's look at two different ways of dealing with a student who has made a mistake.

Example A

Teacher: *Let's look at an argument.*

[Displays and reads]

'Some people believe that giving aid to the poor is counter-productive because it encourages them to be dependent on the rich rather than supporting themselves. However, this view is merely a justification for the selfish rich to keep their money instead of helping the needy. Most people prefer to support themselves, so if they accept charity, they work very hard to reassert their independence. Furthermore, many charity programmes put a great deal of emphasis on helping people to help themselves. So we can see that giving aid to the poor does not necessarily encourage them to be dependent on the rich.' What's the main conclusion of this argument? That is, what is the main thing that the author is trying to persuade us to accept?
Student A: *Is it, 'So we can see that giving aid to the poor does not necessarily encourage them to be dependent on the rich'?*
Teacher: *Why do you think that?*

Student A: *It's the last line, and the reasons about working hard and charities helping the poor to help themselves both support it.*

Teacher: *Yes, the last part of the argument does work like that, well done. Is there another claim in there that is supported by the last line, though?*

Student A: *Oh. I've done it again, haven't I? Confused the main and intermediate conclusions?*

Teacher: *Have you?*

Student A: *Well, now I look at it again, I think the author is showing us that giving aid to the poor doesn't make them dependent so that he can persuade us that the other view is 'merely a justification for the selfish rich'. I think that's how the argument works. But I don't know. I'm confused now. It seems more important to show that charity giving is good than that your opponent is selfish.*

Teacher: *Well, there are two points we could look at. Let's start with selfish opponents. I think quite a lot of us really want to show that people who disagree with us are bad or selfish, so that might be what the author is trying to persuade us to agree with. The other point is about showing 'that charity giving is good'. The author doesn't actually say that.*

Student B: *No, it doesn't say that, but I think A is right, I think it implies that charity giving is good, and there is some support for it. I think that's a conclusion you could draw from the argument.*

Example B

Teacher: *What's the main conclusion of this argument?*

Student A: *Is it, 'So we can see that giving aid to the poor does not necessarily encourage them to be dependent on the rich'?*

Teacher: *No. Anyone else?*

In example A, the teacher uses questioning and modelling to draw out some very high-level thinking from the student who made the mistake, including some thinking about how thinking and reasoning can be structured, and thinking about their own thinking. In example B, the teacher dismisses the answer. It does not matter here that the student is partly right; the answer is branded as wrong, and thinking stops. The answer lies with the teacher, not the student, and this can inhibit the development of high-level thinking skills.

Pay attention to your interventions when students are talking. Which strategies do you use most? How do you feel about not correcting mistakes? If it feels wrong to leave a mistake uncorrected, why does it feel wrong?

Progression towards Student Independence

One of the aims of most thinking courses is for students to become independent thinkers and learners who share control of their learning. The teacher remains in control of the learning environment (refer to Chapter 2), and needs to plan for gradual progression towards student independence. Part of this, as we have discussed, is done by setting frameworks for activities; part by gradually asking students to do more in terms of choosing topics, setting questions, and selecting resources. As we have seen, this can be effective in fully examined courses as well as those that involve assessed research or coursework.

At the beginning of a course it is likely the teacher will choose a topic for students, select materials, ask specific questions to elicit skills, and set a question or task. Students will respond to the stimulus provided.

During the course, students will begin to select their own topics. Perhaps the second topic is negotiated by the whole class. By the third or fourth topic, groups of students might select their own, and in some courses, students might eventually choose a topic individually. This implies that you will need to plan negotiation of topics into your lessons.

During the course, students will also begin to set their own research questions. Perhaps for the second topic the research question can be negotiated by the whole class, with the teacher encouraging students to come up with characteristics of strong research questions they can apply on future occasions. By the third or fourth topic, groups might negotiate research questions with teacher assistance. There will be a need to plan meeting with groups. These can take place during the first thinking period and during the early stages of research.

As the course progresses, students will begin to select their own materials, steadily increasing the number and quality of skills they are able to apply to evaluating and selecting materials. They will gradually analyse, evaluate, reflect, plan, develop reasoning and present reasoning to a higher level. Lesson planning will involve increasing reminders and questions relating to skills covered, and fewer lesson on new skills.

As students become more independent, they may lead more lessons. For example, groups of students may present research proposals including research questions to each other, and evaluate each other's questions. Students may devise games and activities and lead the feedback.

Discussion

What opportunities are there in your course for students to take control of their learning and to become independent? What implications are there for your planning? If students are leading lessons, what implications does this have for planning? What sort of things could go wrong, and how could you deal with them?

What other questions do you have about planning your lessons? Where could you find the answers? Are they in someone else's head, or yours?

5   Resource Planning

The thinking teacher needs to consider a number of questions relating to resources. These include:

- Where can I find good resources?
- What makes a resource good?
- Should I develop my own resources? If so, how?

In this chapter we will first discuss where resources can be found, and what makes a good resource, and then consider whether and how a teacher should develop their own. As in previous chapters, questions and issues will be raised rather than answers provided. There are many different 'right' answers to questions about resources, and the thinking teacher will need to decide which of these possibilities works best in their particular situation. You may find it useful to work through the chapter with your log book, writing down ideas, taking issue with suggestions and thinking through the various possibilities.

Where Can I Find Good Resources?

Good resources for subjects that include a significant element of thinking and reasoning skills can be found in all sorts of places. Because thinking and reasoning skills underlie most school subjects and can be applied to most topical debates, almost any topic can be used. Broadly speaking, so long as it is possible to have and justify an opinion about an issue, that issue can be used to help students develop their thinking and reasoning skills. Some types of source to consider are the following.

- *Textbook:* If possible, use a qualification-specific textbook, even if only as a guide to make sure that specific exam requirements are met. It is not generally wise to use *only* a textbook; although they can guide, they can also limit. Textbooks are written at a fixed point in time and do not change as topical affairs change.

- *Other subject-specific books:* Many of the numerous books in the area of thinking and reasoning skills are aimed too high for students, but it is worth having a library of books to refer to. Always remember to check the contents against the specification or syllabus that you are working with.
- *Newspapers and magazines:* Newspapers and magazines are a valuable source of material for classroom use. They include reports (frequently constructed using evidence), opinion and comment pieces, and reader letters (which are often short, problematic, arguments).
- *Journals:* Some journals can be useful, especially for students embarking on a substantial independent or academic course of study. At the beginning of a thinking course they can be too difficult, as they deal with high-level concepts and complex arguments requiring thinking and reasoning skills that students struggle to get to grips with.
- *Internet:* The internet is a vast source of material of varying quality. Useful sites include the following.

    a) Blogs.
    b) Responses to newspaper comments.
    c) Non-government organisations, including charities. The Red Cross, for example, has some very useful teaching materials which can be adapted for teaching thinking and reasoning skills. Charity websites often include reports, arguments and evidence, as well as campaign materials using more emotive means.
    d) International organisations such as the UN and the ILO. These contain reports, arguments and links to other useful sites.
    e) Portals such as Third World Network. These collect information and links relating to specific areas of interest.
    f) Web searches. These can yield interesting sources on a particular topic – especially useful given that many thinking-and-reasoning-based qualifications also emphasise research skills.
    g) Podcasts.

- *Television and radio programmes:* Although most written examinations are based on written material, there is no reason why audio material should not be used in teaching or in students' individual research. Indeed, listening to complex language and the language of argument can help students to read and write similar language. The most useful programmes include those which involve using debate, argument and evidence to support conclusions.

- *Syllabus/specification:* The syllabus or specification for your qualification is a resource for the teacher which can inform other decisions about resources. How and when to use this to help students to understand the course is an open question (see the discussion in Chapter 1 regarding introducing the course).
- *Information and Communications Technology (ICT) resources:* ICT resources are not essential for effective teaching of thinking skills: as in any subject they need to be used appropriately if they are to enhance students' learning. However, there are three main ways that ICT can support thinking skills and these are considered below.

  1. Students can apply their reasoning skills to other subjects when they undertake assignments involving ICT-based tasks. For example, in history they could carry out internet research, and assess the credibility of web sources to help them judge whether or not the material they have found is reliable historical evidence. Subject-related or critical-thinking discussion groups can be set up using the institution's intranet, with fresh topics posted regularly by the tutor.
  2. Industry-standard ICT packages can be used to support the teaching of thinking skills or critical thinking. For example, students could word process their answers to a 'round robin reasoning' activity (see Chapter 7, page 141), or use presentation software to help communicate an argument or case verbally to the group. Interactive whiteboard applications can enhance critical thinking lessons. Possible activities are:

     a) gap-filling (cloze) tasks where students insert argument indicator words in an argument;
     b) argument analysis using colours for different components e.g. blue for reasons and red for conclusions (see page 63).

  3. ICT can be used to support teaching of thinking skills and critical thinking through the use of purpose-designed software and learning packages. Popular packages available at the time of writing are listed in Chapter 9, but generally they fall into two categories:

a) Courses, either online or on DVD, that support teaching of the subject content or just provide practice questions, usually multiple choice. Typically, such packages deal best with assumptions, evidence, credibility, flaws and fallacies.

b) Argument-mapping software available in various versions, including versions for specialist tasks, such as mapping legal arguments. Some teachers find that teaching students the skill of producing diagrammatic representations of argument structures helps them to understand and analyse arguments and advocate the use of argument-mapping software. Many students rapidly learn to use this type of software and enjoy doing so. A number of these packages were developed in Australia by Austhink, and are now marketed in other countries. Whether it is worth purchasing such software is a matter of choice: paper and pen are unexciting but cheap and cheerful, not technology-dependent and probably what students will have to use in any public examination. An alternative is standard word-processing or drawing software, but students can be distracted if they are not skilled at using it.

Remember that ICT does not replace face-to-face discussion, or teacher–student interaction.

- *Exam papers and mark schemes:* It goes without saying that specimen and past exam papers and mark schemes are valuable resources. They can be used as exam practice, in peer assessment to give students an understanding of how the examiner thinks and as a guide to how to answer specific types of question.

  Past exam papers can also show what sort of topics are likely to be discussed in the exam, and at what level. Some qualifications use topical issues from the media using authentic materials written by, for example, journalists, others tend to use well-discussed general subjects such as school holidays or prisons written or significantly manipulated by examiners. If the qualification you are working on emphasises topical issues in context, it would be well to prepare students using topical news items, and thinking beyond a specific news article to the context. For example, OCR Critical Thinking A2 uses authentic opinion and argument pieces from newspapers and magazines. The candidates who do best in the examination have an awareness that the piece was written in a context rather than in isolation. The specification does not specify particular general knowledge, but candidates who are familiar with current affairs tend to respond in a more thoughtful way to the arguments in the examination than those for whom a particular argument exists in a vacuum.

- *Examiner reports:* Examiner reports are published by awarding bodies on their websites. They often talk about candidate performance, and give examples of answers which gained marks and answers which did not. It is worth checking these reports to make sure you are preparing your candidates thoroughly for the demands of the examination.
- *Exam board websites:* Most exam boards have a teacher support forum on their website. These often include lesson plans and resource materials.
- *Other teachers:* Other teachers can be a good source of resource materials and ideas, as well as providing a support network. Remember to check materials before using them though – discovering towards the end of a lesson that the questions on the worksheet you have handed out can't be answered is a painful experience!

 ## Sources to Investigate

The list below is not exhaustive, but the authors have found these websites useful starting points when hunting for ideas, for resource preparation, as well as for writing examination papers.

- The BBC website is good for informative and readable articles, which rarely contain sustained reasoning, but offer topical ideas, especially on health, science and technology. The religion and ethics page has links to past programmes from the *Moral Maze* and message board posts are well worth looking at if you want material containing reasoning flaws. See www.bbc.co.uk and also www.bbc.co.uk/worldservice.
- Ben Goldacre's 'Bad Science' column, printed in the *Guardian*, downloadable at www.guardian.co.uk/science/series/badscience, is informative concerning the misdemeanours of pharmaceutical companies, flawed research and misleading scientific journalism.
- *New Scientist* is also useful for articles on science topics, particularly the short articles and the editorial – see www.newscientist.com. Only a limited amount of *New Scientist* is available free, but it is

worth buying the magazine from time to time. Many school and college libraries keep it for science students.

- *The New York Times* – www.nytimes.com.
- The *Economist* for world affairs, economics and business with an international perspective – not as heavy as it sounds – at www.economist.com.
- *New Statesman* for articles on politics, world affairs, society and culture – www.newstatesman.com.
- *Straits Times* at www.straitstimes.com – for a perspective from south-east Asia.
- *Pravda*, the Russian newspaper site, has interesting articles from a post-communist perspective (if you have no objection to clunky translations and a surfeit of curvaceous females) – see http://english.pravda.ru.
- Al-jazeera – http://english.aljazeera.net/. Qatar-based international news and current affairs channel.
- *The Times* – www.timesonline.co.uk. UK newspaper (subscriber access only). The *Guardian* and *Independent* sometimes give alternative views.
- *Daily Mail* – www.dailymail.co.uk. Can be a very good source of arguments employing numerous rhetorical and emotional tricks.
- *Mail* and *Guardian* www.mg.co.za South African news and opinion.
- *New Zealand Herald* – www.nzherald.co.nz. Offers a New Zealand perspective on news.
- *Jakarta Post* – www.thejakartapost.com. Asian view from Indonesia.
- *Bangkok Post* – www.bangkokpost.com/news. From Thailand.
- *New Straits Times* – www.nst.com.my. Malaysian source.
- *Pakistan Dawn* – www.dawn.com. View from Pakistan.
- *Asia Times* – www.atimes.com. Hong Kong-based.
- *Times of India* – www.timesofindia.indiatimes.com. From India. Useful comment and blogs.
- *China Daily* – www.chinadaily.com.cn/opinion. From China, its strongly Chinese perspective can challenge those of us rooted in a Western or even post-colonial perspective.
- *Scientific American* – www.scientificamerican.com. This publication takes a scientific and technological perspective. Look out also for *Scientific American Mind*.
- Oxfam – www.oxfam.org. Charity site that includes reports, appeals and some arguments.
- United Nations – www.un.org/en. In addition to documents relating to the organisation itself, the website includes news,

reviews, global issues, resources and reports. There are sections on Peace and Security, Development, Human Rights, Humanitarian Affairs and International Law.

- Red Cross – www.redcross.org.uk/education. Charity website that includes some very good teaching resources emphasising the importance of thinking through an issue. Could easily be adapted for use in a course with a significant element of thinking and reasoning skills.
- Sociolingo's Africa – www.sociolingo.com. A blog run by someone with a background in sociolinguistics and education, this includes useful resources relating to Africa. Some are rather challenging and students may need help in navigating the site.
- Third World Network – www.twnside.org.sg. 'Third World Network is an independent, non-profit international network of organisations and individuals involved in issues relating to development, Third World and North–South affairs' according to their website. Again, some of the content is fairly academic.
- Websites and blogs run by self-proclaimed 'sceptics' are worth trying for off-the-wall topics. These often – but not always – involve flawed reasoning, poor use of evidence and ranting.

Discussion

Which of these resources do you already use? Which might you think of using in future? What other resources could you add to the list? Do you regularly find new materials, or generally reuse the same materials as last year? Why?

What Makes a Resource Good?

A good resource is one that allows the thinking teacher to meet the aims and objectives for the course and lesson. A report or short factual piece (either written or audio) might, for example, be the starting point for a lesson or research project. A report can be differentiated from argument, facts being used to stimulate a discussion and prompt more research. However, thinking and reasoning skills require reasoning (a thread of persuasive thought connected in a logical manner) and argument (a specific form of reasoning that uses reasons to support a conclusion), so a significant proportion of the materials you use should contain reasoning and argument.

Which topics are suitable?

One of the attractions of a thinking skills course is that teachers and students can investigate and argue about issues, topics and contexts which interest them. The examination syllabus or specification defines the skills to be tested, but not usually the content. Even where topics are listed in the syllabus, such as for IGCSE Global Perspectives and Pre-U Global Perspectives and Independent Research Report, the teacher and student have a great deal of freedom to decide what precisely is studied within that topic.

This means that almost any topic can be suitable; very few need be off limits. The question for the thinking teacher is how to treat these. Overly teacher-determined, fact-based treatments of a topic are less likely to encourage students to develop their thinking and reasoning skills than questioning, investigative treatments.

The IGCSE Global Perspectives syllabus, for example, lists 'water' as a topic. A factual treatment of this topic, whereby students learn about the physical geography of rivers, the means of cleaning water and the world distribution of wet and arid areas is unlikely to be productive. An investigation into why water matters, what problems there are regarding water, how serious these problems are and how they might best be solved is more likely to encourage students to develop their thinking and reasoning skills. Alternatively, parts of the overall issue could be discussed, such as, 'Is it reasonable for rich people in dry countries to have swimming pools?' or 'Should water be used for growing flowers in Kenya to be sold in Western countries?'

GCE A2 Critical Thinking and Pre-U Global Perspectives and Independent Research Report both require candidates to be able to reason ethically and see issues from an ethical perspective. Knowing what certain key philosophers have said is much less important in these qualifications than being able to reason ethically. So the topic, 'What Bentham and Mill said about Utilitarianism' is less useful than a discussion on the topic, 'To what extent is it right to torture suspected terrorists to gain information?' The latter can include a consideration of the question, 'How do we decide what is right?', allowing students to think through issues rather than simply telling them what key philosophers thought.

Who decides the topics?

As we have discussed, there is a role in many thinking courses for students to determine their own topics. At the beginning of the course, the teacher may choose, whereas later, students can play a greater role. The teacher may pick a general topic and allow students to select an aspect that interests them. Alternatively, groups of students could be given the task of reading the newspapers and choosing two or three issues/articles that appeal to them. The class could then vote on which is studied. If students are shy of suggesting ideas, then perhaps there could be an anonymous list.

How serious do the topics have to be?

Given the choice, students may well opt for rather frivolous issues, but there is nothing wrong with this. Indeed, you may sometimes choose less serious issues yourself, both to motivate students and to enliven discussion. Students can effectively develop their reasoning skills when talking about popular music or films, for example. Allowing them to argue and reason about subjects they are familiar with may make them more willing to really debate rather than merely collect information or repeat earlier thoughts.

'Big' topics such as abortion, the environment or climate change are often so familiar that students groan 'not this again', and then trot out their preconceptions rather than consider the issues from different perspectives or react to arguments presented to them. By this stage of education they may be thoroughly bored by over-familiar topics, so consider approaching these from an unusual perspective that will challenge students to think fresh, independent thoughts.

Another possibility is to deal with serious topics, but not those that students have repeatedly covered. Until students have developed sufficient maturity, topics that arouse deeply held political, cultural or religious values may be rather dangerous ground, and should be treated with care. However, one of the aims of many of the thinking courses under discussion is to help students go beyond their original perspectives and challenge their own preconceptions. By questioning and developing their ideas they will develop maturity.

In conclusion, it is worth keeping a balance between serious and frivolous subjects. Students need to be introduced to a range of big and trivial issues, but also allowed to follow their interests.

Discussion
What sort of topics are usually discussed in your lessons? Do you stick to issues where you have some knowledge? Why? Are there any topics you would not be prepared to discuss in your lessons? How much freedom do you give students to choose topics? Why? How confident are you in questioning students in appropriate ways on material they have found for themselves?

Should I Develop My Own Resources?

Developing good materials for teaching and assessing any subject requires time and effort. This is especially so with thinking skills, partly because there is a tension between the imprecision of everyday speech and writing and the precision needed to think critically. So why take the trouble to develop original teaching resources for your thinking skills classes? If for no other reason, it is worth doing because course materials that reflect your own students' needs and interests can empower them much more than those aimed at non-specific students.

On a more pragmatic level, there is a lack of good teaching resources for thinking and reasoning skills, particularly compared with longer-established subjects. You are likely to need extra materials to sustain your students' interest throughout the course. Lessons that were successful with last year's group won't necessarily work this year. Sticking with the textbook is a secure option if you lack confidence in your ability to teach thinking skills, but will limit the extent to which students can explore 'live', topical issues or pursue topics that spark their interest. Furthermore, most current resources are designed for teaching critical thinking in isolation rather than the full range of thinking and reasoning skills embedded in a context.

Crucially, producing original resources, alongside discussion and working with other teachers in subject communities, helps the teacher develop specialist subject expertise. Analysing and evaluating the argument in a passage sharpens the teacher's own critical thinking far more effectively than accepting textbook answers – which are not necessarily the only possible interpretation of the text.

If you do not enjoy writing materials, or have insufficient time to produce detailed resource materials from scratch, don't worry. Materials are increasingly available, and your own resource production will mostly involve adapting material from the media. Your main role will be writing questions rather than writing whole articles or arguments.

Alternatively, if you really hate developing materials, but have a colleague who loves doing so but hates, say, administration, you might be able to share responsibilities.

Discussion

Do you enjoy producing materials? Why? Which aspects of material production do you find most satisfying? If you do not enjoy it, why not? Are you simply lacking confidence, or do your strengths lie elsewhere? Remember to think through your strengths as well as areas where you lack confidence, and remember that lack of confidence is not the same as lack of ability. Do you produce materials for your other subjects? What skills do you use for this, and are they transferable?

How Do I Develop My Own Resources?

Developing your own resources comes under two categories:

1. Writing materials from scratch.
2. Using materials from the media, including print, audio and internet.

Writing material from scratch

If you have sufficient imagination, time, and enthusiasm, writing your own passages is gratifying. If you do this, remember to consider the aims and objectives you are trying to meet, and ensure the material achieves these. It is easy to get carried away with enthusiasm about the subject matter and forget to build in opportunities for candidates to use their thinking and reasoning skills.

If you are writing an argument, check there is a stated conclusion and reasons offered in support of this. It is good practice to analyse the argument before using it; it will help you to identify any problems before your students do.

If you are writing flawed reasoning, double and triple check the flaws are actually there. During lessons, be prepared for students to interpret the reasoning in a different way. When you have written material yourself, it is much harder to see why a student interprets it in a different light than if someone else has written it. Remember to ask students to explain their thinking.

Consider the length and language demands of the piece you're writing. Long articles with demanding language can put some students off, or distract them from the skills they are practising.

Consider whether you are making the most efficient use of your time. Writing source material is difficult and time consuming, so it might be better in some cases to concentrate on adapting material from the media, including radio, television, the internet and the press. Don't be put off by the difficulties, though – sometimes it is best to write your own materials.

Using materials from the media including print, audio and internet

There are many advantages to adapting material from the media. It can:

- improve candidates' general knowledge and ability to think about current affairs;
- prepare candidates for examinations in which real materials are used, and for research using real materials from the media;
- help candidates to bear the context of an argument in mind rather than seeing it as an isolated, disjointed piece of text.

Using real material has the further advantage that you may come across a useful idea, programme or text whilst engaging in everyday, relaxing activities such as reading the newspaper, listening to the radio or watching TV.

We will consider:

- finding suitable stimulus material;
- turning stimulus material into usable lesson material;
- suggestions for activities based on stimulus material.

Finding suitable stimulus material

When you are looking for material you need to consider complexity, length, nature and variety of the stimuli you use.

How complex should stimulus material be?

The complexity of stimulus material will depend on the stage of the course, the ability of the students, and the aims and objectives of the lesson. At the beginning of a course there is a case for using simple print or audio texts to allow students to focus on the thinking skills rather than the content. At other times there is a case for introducing complex texts; students might, for example, practise identifying a conclusion in a complex text. Alternatively, they could discuss the different perspectives of participants in a complex TV debate, or identify where participants are using argument or other kinds of reasoning.

Be aware that complex tasks on complex material at the beginning of a course can put students off. Be aware also that some able students might feel insulted by simplistic stimulus material. However, complex thinking can come from simple situations, such as the decision about what Donna should do in Lesson Idea One in Chapter 1 (see pages 9–18).

How long should the stimulus material be?

Stimulus material can vary from a single word, such as 'value', 'freedom' or 'terrorist', to a film or a book. Most of the stimulus material you use will come between these extremes. A great deal can be gained from a short passage, such as:

> The average farmer calls in the vet to their livestock more frequently than they visit the doctor for their own health problems. It is evident that farmers care more for the welfare of their livestock than their own. Animal rights activists are misguided in their criticisms of farming and should turn their attention to a different target.

In general, it is worth avoiding very long stimulus material, especially at the beginning of a course, and especially if it is also complex. During the course you will need to use your judgement to begin introducing longer, more complex source material.

What sort of stimulus material should I use?

As we have discussed, almost any kind of material can be used, so long as you adapt your questioning to suit your aims and objectives. In general, material containing argument, debate, reasoning, opinions and evidence is likely to be most useful in developing thinking and reasoning skills.

The key here is to be aware of the nature of the material you are using, and what sort of activity it's suitable for. A common mistake is to call journalistic reports 'arguments' even though they employ no real argument. If you're using a report, call it a report. And don't ask students to find the main conclusion of a passage if there isn't one.

Let's say you want to use a documentary in your lesson. Does the documentary have a conclusion? Is it an argument? Does it contain a series of mini-arguments? Does it use evidence well or jump to conclusions, speculating on the basis of a tiny amount of evidence? How much evidence would be necessary to properly support the conclusions drawn in the documentary?

Should I vary the kinds of stimulus material I use?

Yes. Avoid the temptation to stick to the tried and trusted; students will benefit most from diverse stimulus material. Consider the perspectives presented in the material, including different opinions, different kinds of reasoning and fundamentally different worldviews. You could use various newspapers (including some from abroad), web responses to newspaper articles, blogs, a radio discussion, a political speech, an advert, and so forth. In each case, you and your students could consider the different kinds of reasoning used for specific purposes, and set arguments into their broader context.

At a later stage in the course, comparing arguments from different sources helps foster a critically questioning attitude and the ability to evaluate different perspectives.

Once you have found a suitable passage, the checklist below will help you identify some activities to develop reasoning skills. There are, of course, other activities that will develop thinking and reasoning skills; this is merely a guide.

Material that ...	can be used to get students to ...
contains an argument, which may be just within one paragraph	– find the argument by looking for argument indicator words such as 'therefore' or 'should' for the conclusion, 'because' or 'as' for a reason
presents evidence, including evidence in the form of images, graphs and tables	– draw possible inferences – offer explanations for the evidence – assess the relevance of the evidence
interprets evidence	– determine whether the evidence supports the interpretation – suggest alternative interpretations
uses evidence to make recommendations	– assess whether the evidence is strong enough to support the recommendation
quotes two or three different sources	– assess and compare the credibility of sources
presents two or three different perspectives	– consider how far one perspective supports or challenges another perspective
contains weaknesses in reasoning, including flaws such as slippery slope	– identify weaknesses and name flaws – evaluate the effect of weaknesses on the strength of the reasoning; does this weakness mean that the author has not supported the conclusion? – rewrite weak reasoning to provide stronger grounds for accepting the conclusion – produce a counter-argument
includes any of the above	– research the topic to produce further arguments on an aspect of the issue

Turning stimulus material into usable lesson material

Once you have chosen your stimulus material check that it is accessible, fit for purpose and will allow you to meet your aims and objectives. If you have second thoughts, and decide it's too hard, you have several options:

- save it for a later stage in the course;
- simplify it, perhaps by removing complex vocabulary or inserting argument indicator words such as 'therefore';
- use only part of it;
- structure your lesson so that the topic material and/or language are introduced in a simpler form;
- don't use it at all.

Beyond this, you need to consider the following questions:

- What am I aiming to achieve with this material?
- Where does it fit in the lesson plan?
- What questions and activities can I devise to use with this material?
- How much flexibility is there for responding to students' needs?

We will consider these questions in the next two subsections.

Value – version 1

Objectives:

- To encourage students to question and clarify terms.
- To encourage students to question their own preconceptions.

Activities:

- Give students two minutes to write down everything they can think of relating to value.
- Ask students to discuss in groups what they thought.

Class discussion:

- Did every student think the same things?
- What were the areas of similarity and difference?

Class/group activity:

- Make a visual diagram of the different associations of the word value.

- If necessary, stimulate discussion by writing up the following:

   I value my dog.
   I value my freedom.
   I value people's houses.
   We must stick to traditional family values.
   Are all these uses of 'value' the same?

- Ask, 'How important is it that we all value the same things?' or 'Does it matter whether we have any values?' or 'Are my values more important than her values?'
- Discuss these issues, asking how different understandings of 'value' arising from the earlier discussion affect the arguments students produce.
- Ask students to write an argument to support their view, making sure they clarify their understanding of 'value' and respond to different perspectives.

Here, the stimulus material is used right at the beginning of the lesson plan, and the various activities are fairly flexible. It would be possible to follow student interests and thoughts. If students queried Western values or Christian/Muslim/Hindu values it would be possible to allow them to discuss/research these particular values. It is important that students write an argument by the end of the lesson, putting the questioning they have done into practice, but the precise route to arrive there is not important.

Value – version 2
Objectives:

- To introduce ethical reasoning.
- Students should begin to think in an ethical way.

Activities:
Discussion and questions:

- Where do our values come from?
- Elicit example of values and how students think that they know them.
- Compare ideas about values coming from God, family, education, and discuss whether they are absolute or relative.
- Does it matter whether values are absolute or relative? Use examples to contextualise the abstract issues being discussed – for example (female) circumcision, wearing a veil, killing a person.
- How do we know what is right?

- Compare ideas about the right action leading to the best consequences versus an action being right or wrong in itself. Elicit examples.
- Is there a connection between our values and what is right? Use a comparison between the Resistance in France during the Second World War and terrorists today.

Again, the stimulus of value comes towards the beginning of the lesson. The lesson is fairly flexible, but there is a clear direction the teacher wants it to take to ensure that students have thought through specific issues.

We can see here how the same, one-word stimulus can lead to two completely different lessons if the aims of the lesson are different.

Farmers, vets and animal rights activists
Stimulus:

> The average farmer calls in the vet to their livestock more frequently than they visit the doctor for their own health problems. It is evident that farmers care more for the welfare of their livestock than their own. Animal rights activists are misguided in their criticisms of farming and should turn their attention to a different target.

Objectives:

- To revise identifying a conclusion.
- To consider the strength of an argument.
- To research animal rights issues.

Activities:

- Discuss students' existing views about animal rights and animal rights activists.
- Begin to frame the discussion that will lead to the research project.
- Elicit from students a definition of argument, and how to identify a conclusion.
- Ask students to underline the conclusion in this argument.
- Discuss whether the whole of the last sentence is the main conclusion, or merely the last phrase. (There is some room for interpretation here, but it would be possible to insert 'therefore' in the sentence: 'Animal rights activists are misguided in their criticisms of farming; they should therefore turn their attention to a different target.' This indicates that only the last phrase is the main conclusion, and the first part of the sentence is an intermediate conclusion.)

Ask students what they think of the argument; is it strong? Elicit answers suggesting that:

- farmers generally have hundreds of animals, so it is likely the vet will be required more often than the doctor; thus it doesn't follow that farmers care more for their animals than for themselves;
- farmers might need to call the vet out for their animals because of the poor conditions in which they keep them;
- even if farmers do care more for their animals than for themselves, this does not mean that animal rights activists are misguided in their criticisms of farming, especially not if their criticisms are directed at farming practices rather than how much farmers care about animals;
- so it doesn't follow that animal rights activists should turn their attention to a different target.

Set up a research project, reminding students that they need to be aware of what they are being persuaded to accept (conclusions) and any weaknesses in the reasoning they find.

In this case, the stimulus material comes after a context has been set and students have been introduced to key terms in the discussion. This lesson is less flexible than the two about values, as there are clear stages in a thinking process that needs to be completed to give students the tools to begin the research project. The teacher will therefore need to be stricter about encouraging a particular way of thinking rather than allowing students to follow their own thoughts.

Discussion
What would you do differently in the examples given of developing lessons from simple source material? Why?

Consider the following situation, which occurred in summer 2009. A Muslim woman wanted to go swimming in her hotel in France, but the pool guard would not let her swim because hotel policy did not allow full-length swimming costumes. The woman went to the press and there was a lively international debate about the issues involved.

How would you use this situation as a stimulus? Would you (or your students) find press reports and arguments about it? Would you discuss the ethics? Would you consider the possible consequences of each person's action? Would you use the situation to tease out different perspectives? How? How would your lesson relate to your aims and objectives?

Part 2

Tools for Enriching Achievement

Introduction to Part 2

Part 1 of this Toolkit is designed to enable you to survive if you are thrown in at the deep end as a teacher of thinking skills. Once you have got through the first weeks of the course, you may want to take stock. Part 2 provides tools for enriching achievement. These will help you review strategies, consider alternatives and build on good practice. It outlines the background to current approaches to thinking and reasoning skills and the benefits for students. It also looks at ways of integrating thinking skills into other curriculum subjects.

6 Background and Benefits

What are Thinking Skills and Critical Thinking?

Most teachers and education professionals accept unquestioningly that 'thinking skills' and 'critical thinking' are positive attributes which should be cultivated in learners, but they would be pushed to give a clear explanation of what these terms mean. The confusion is understandable and justifiable: the literature on critical thinking is characterised by 'a pervasive miasma of overlapping uses of such terms as skill, process, procedure, behaviour, mental operations etc.' (Bailin *et al.*, 1999, p 269).

For a start, 'thinking skills', 'higher thinking skills', 'reflective thinking', 'critical thinking', 'problem solving' and 'reasoning' are not strictly synonymous, though they are certainly related concepts. However, they are often used loosely, as interchangeable labels. Furthermore, the term 'critical thinking' means different things to different disciplines. In the study of English literature, it is applied to the evaluation of literary texts; in philosophy the focus is on logic and reasoning; for the pedagogical theorist or psychologist it may suggest reflecting about learning – metacognition. All of these elements are pertinent to the teaching of thinking skills and critical thinking, but the different strands need unpicking.

None of this need have impinged on most subject teachers' classroom practice had it not been that, in response to technological change and globalisation, many governments are implementing policies that encourage teaching programmes (some of which are outlined in this chapter) aimed at promoting students' 'thinking skills' or 'critical thinking' in the secondary phase of education. In England and Wales, for example, interest in thinking skills as a means of enriching the 16–19 curriculum (plus a favourable funding regime) contributed to Critical Thinking becoming the fastest growing GCE Advanced Subsidiary examination subject in 2007. With 25,000 candidates, mainly from year 12, it was ahead of well-established subjects such as music, business and economics. As a result, many post-16 teachers have found themselves preparing students for public examinations in thinking skills or critical thinking as a discrete subject, even though they have neither qualifications in the subject nor professional training to teach it.

This chapter explains first what the wider thinking skills are, and then considers critical thinking and problem solving. Key theoretical approaches are outlined to help the non-specialist understand the rationale for different approaches to teaching thinking and reasoning skills. There are snapshots of different countries' approaches, and the benefits and advantages of introducing a thinking skills programme are considered.

Thinking skills programmes and approaches

The definition of *thinking skills* produced by Valerie Wilson for the Scottish Council for Research in Education (Wilson, 2000, page 7) has the merit of clarity and simplicity, and has been recognised by UK Government education departments. *Thinking* is the process of cognition, knowing, remembering, perceiving and attending; *skills* are the acts of collecting and sorting information; analysing, drawing conclusions, brainstorming, problem solving, evaluating options, planning, monitoring, decision making and reflecting. 'Thinking skills' are simply a way of looking at the problem.

Following a review of thinking skills carried out in 1999 (McGuinness, 1999), the UK Department for Education and Skills adopted the approach that thinking skills consist of information processing, reasoning, enquiry, creative thinking and evaluation. Other frameworks – and there are many[8] – have categorised thinking skills as critical thinking, creative thinking, problem solving and decision making. Whichever framework is preferred, critical thinking, problem solving and creative thinking cannot satisfactorily be regarded as discrete operations, or defined as processes isolated from each other. Whilst psychologists and philosophers continue to investigate and debate the relationship between thinking skills at a metacognitive level (being aware of and understanding the ways they could be used to tackle a task) and at a cognitive level (being able to undertake a task), for teachers of thinking skills it is enough to know that thinking skills programmes fall broadly into two categories.

First, there are programmes designed to *extend students' cognition*; that is, creative thinking, reasoning (or critical thinking) skills, problem solving and decision making. The focus of this book is the teaching of cognitive thinking skills, in particular reasoning and problem solving.

Second, there are programmes intended to *develop students' metacognition*. Briefly, metacognition is the ability to plan, describe and evaluate one's own thinking and learning. It operates on two levels:

first, the acquisition of metacognitive knowledge, and then being able to produce it, which develops over time. Most teachers would accept that students with greater metacognitive awareness outperform those with less. Metacognitive strategies focus on connecting new information to former knowledge; deliberately selecting thinking strategies; and planning, monitoring and evaluating thinking processes. A key benefit of a course in thinking and reasoning skills is that students start to think about their thinking and thus improve it.

Discussion

Which of the thinking and reasoning skills will be targeted in the course you are teaching? Will the course address a number of skills, or focus on one or two? How does this affect the way you teach?

What is critical thinking?

As we have seen, critical thinking is one of the wider set of cognitive thinking skills, which also includes creative thinking, problem solving and decision making. This section provides a brief history of critical thinking as a discipline and looks at some of the definitions of critical thinking that leading thinking skills researchers have produced. Common misconceptions about critical thinking will also be considered.

The related disciplines of thinking skills and critical thinking originated in the work of John Dewey, whose interests bridged philosophy, psychology and education. Dewey developed the concept of *reflective thinking*. For Dewey, learning from experience, doing (problem solving) and reflecting on that experience were central concepts. Dewey's definition of reflective thinking was 'active, persistent, and careful consideration of any belief or supposed form of knowledge in the light of the grounds that support it and the further conclusion to which it tends' (Dewey, 1909, p. 9). Donald Schön, amongst others, extended Dewey's theories, with the result that many professional training routes (including teaching, medicine and nursing) encourage reflection on one's own professional practice.

Discussion

Go back to the notes you made in your log book as you read Section 1 – they constitute reflective thinking on your own professional practice. How far has this process had a positive impact on your classroom practice?

After the Second World War, Reuven Feuerstein, a child psychologist who had studied with Piaget, began work in Israel with child survivors of the Holocaust. Feuerstein's contention is that children's intelligence can be modified by teaching them thinking skills. Through his system of Instrumental Enrichment he achieves impressive results among children with emotional and behavioural difficulties. Children's problem solving and analytical thinking are enhanced, and strategies developed that could be applied to life.

Discussion
What do you think? From your experience, how far can students' intelligence be modified by teaching them thinking skills? Jot down your own observations as evidence.

Historically, US universities have dominated work on thinking skills. Professor Robert Sternberg of Yale University established a definition of critical thinking that significantly influenced subsequent work: 'Critical Thinking comprises the mental processes, strategies, and representations people use to solve problems, make decisions, and learn new concepts' (Sternberg, 1986, p. 2). Sternberg's definition and approach was one amongst a number developed by US academics. Faced with the confusing variety of approaches to thinking skills, the Committee on Pre-College Philosophy of the American Philosophical Association convened a panel of sixty US and Canadian academics and teachers from backgrounds in philosophy, psychology and education. They conducted an analysis of critical thinking skills, and extended it to consider the *dispositions* of the critical thinker. The outcome was the 'Delphi Report' (after the methodology), including Facione's definition and a detailed exposition of the disposition of the critical thinker.

Given the size of the committee, the level of detail in the definition and lengthy list of the characteristics of critical thinkers are perhaps unsurprising. Critical thinking was:

> ... purposeful, self-regulatory judgement which results in interpretation, analysis, evaluation, and inference, as well as explanation of the evidential, conceptual, methodological, criteriological, or contextual considerations upon which that judgement is based. CT is essential as a tool of inquiry. As such, CT is a liberating force in education and a powerful resource in one's personal and civic life. While not synonymous with good thinking, CT is a pervasive and self-rectifying human phenomenon. The ideal critical thinker is habitually inquisitive, well-informed,

trustful of reason, open-minded, flexible, fair-minded in evaluation, honest in facing personal biases, prudent in making judgements, willing to reconsider, clear about issues, orderly in complex matters, diligent in seeking relevant information, reasonable in the selection of criteria, focused in inquiry, and persistent in seeking results which are as precise as the subject and the circumstances of inquiry permit. (Facione, 1990)

Where the Delphi Report broke new ground was in stressing the importance of education in nurturing the dispositions of the critical thinker, as well as the skills.

Robert H. Ennis produced a thankfully shorter and simpler definition: 'Critical Thinking is reasonable, reflective thinking that is focused on deciding what to believe' (Ennis, 1996, www.criticalthinking.net).

The emphasis on the disposition of the critical thinker – the emotional dimension – was taken further by some protagonists, such as Richard Paul and Linda Elder at the Centre for Critical Thinking affiliated to Sonoma State University (see www.criticalthinking.org), who focus on publishing materials aimed at helping teachers design classroom activities that encourage emotional intelligence in relationships through the development of critical thinking. For some teachers, this approach may not be entirely comfortable, but the practical thrust of the work at Sonoma – emphasising that critical thinking is a tool for use in everyday relationships, decision making, life in general and other academic studies – has been reflected in work done in the UK. Alec Fisher and Michael Scriven's *Critical Thinking* was a key work which emerged from the University of East Anglia Centre for Research in Critical Thinking. They focused on critical thinking as a practical tool that recognises the inadequacy of language, and defined it as 'skilled and active interpretation and evaluation of observations and communications, information and argumentation' (Fisher and Scriven, 1997, p. 21).

The emphasis of most theoretical work outlined above has been on critical thinking as a set of generic skills or abilities. In contrast, John McPeck contended that critical thinking was domain- or subject-specific, does not exist in isolation, and cannot be taught as a discrete subject. For McPeck, critical thinking was 'conceptually and practically empty' (McPeck, 1981). The resultant debate – over whether thinking skills can be taught in isolation or only through subject specialisms – has since moved on from what seemed to be polarised positions. Most researchers and practitioners would accept that different approaches can be successful, depending on the teaching situation and factors such as the age of the students. This discussion and its implications are explored in Chapter 7.

From a classroom practitioner's point of view, the work of Diane Halpern is of major significance. In *Critical Thinking across the Curriculum: A Brief Edition of Thought and Knowledge* (Halpern, 1997), she applied theories and research from cognitive psychology to produce practical guidance on the development of critical thinking and learning skills.

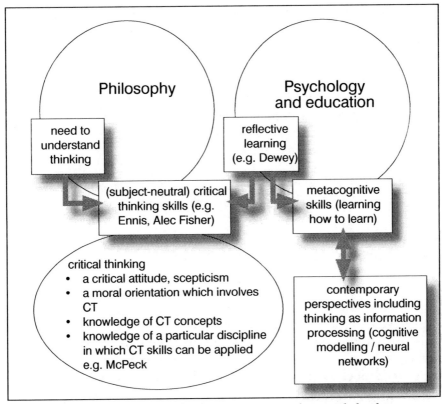

Simplified representation of the development of critical thinking

Debate about what constitutes critical thinking looks set to continue. Given the multiplicity of definitions in existence, one wonders why the UK's Qualifications and Curriculum Authority saw the necessity to produce another, but it duly convened its own committee of subject specialists. (One of the authors of this text was amongst the guilty.) QCA defined critical thinking as 'a form of reflective reasoning which analyses and evaluates information and arguments by applying a range of intellectual skills in order to reach clear, logical and coherent judgements within a given context' (QCA, 2003). The reference to 'intellectual skills' reflects QCA's role as a regulatory authority grappling with the relatively untried assessment of critical thinking skills.

Not to be outdone, Cambridge Assessment (the international public examination board wholly owned by Cambridge University) subsequently produced its own definition, which specifies the skills that make up critical thinking. Critical thinking is:

> the analytical thinking which underlies all rational discourse and enquiry. It is characterised by a meticulous and rigorous approach. As an academic discipline, it is unique in that it explicitly focuses on the processes involved in being rational. These processes include:
>
> - analysing arguments
> - judging the relevance and significance of information
> - evaluating claims, inferences, arguments and explanations
> - constructing clear and coherent arguments
> - forming well-reasoned judgements and decisions.
>
> Being rational also requires an open-minded yet critical approach to one's own thinking as well as that of others. (Black, 2008, p. 33)

Misconceptions about critical thinking

When teachers are setting up a thinking skills or critical thinking course, they often encounter colleagues' misconceptions and assumptions (in the everyday sense) about what critical thinking is, and what it is not. This section will enable you to deal with common objections to the introduction of thinking skills and determine whether any concerns you have are justified. Some of the commonest objections are:

- *We can't teach them to think.* The final section of this chapter will explain the benefits – including improved thinking – that students gain from a critical thinking course. The online supplement (online) lists some of the academic research that provides evidence against this claim.
- *They can think anyway.* Indeed, they *can* think already. They can probably write essays already too, but we carry on giving them guidance on and practice in essay technique in the belief that it will help them produce better essays. We would not expect talented musicians or sportspeople to be successful in their chosen field without practice. However good you are at something, you need to practise it to become excellent – and even the least fit person can become more athletic with practice. Likewise, following a suitable thinking skills or critical thinking

course will enable students to think more effectively, in ways that are different to their routine thinking – and also to write better essays.

- *Critical thinking is no more than a formulaic and mechanistic approach to analysis of argument.* It has to be acknowledged that overuse of 'scaffolding' in a critical thinking course can result in an intellectually arid approach, but this is not what the subject is about.

Critical thinking is, above all, applying criteria (standards) to thinking but, as Facione noted, 'Not every useful cognitive process should be thought of as CT. Not every valuable thinking skill is CT skill. CT is one among a family of closely related forms of higher-order thinking, along with, for example, problem solving, decision making and creative thinking' (Facione, 1990). We will consider in detail some of the things that critical thinking *isn't* in the sections that follow.

What critical thinking isn't

- *Critical thinking is not argumentativeness.* Neither, though, is it negative criticism, although critical thinking techniques are sometimes misused in deliberately destructive ways. Such misuse breaches the critical thinker's *principle of charity*, which states that the critical thinker should treat another person's argument as being based on reason, and not intentionally seek to interpret it as irrational. The good critical thinker aims to assess the relative strengths of their own and others' reasoning, and does not pick out weaknesses alone. Equally, critical thinking is not purely skill in using the *language* of argumentation in essay and report writing. It is entirely possible to sprinkle argument indicators, such as 'since', 'therefore', 'thus' and 'in conclusion' through a piece of work, without having constructed a sound, reasoned argument.
- *Critical thinking is not lack of emotion:* Critical thinking is not an absence of emotion, although it may involve taking emotions into account and should help better understanding of the impact that emotions can have on another person's perspective on a situation.
- *Critical thinking is not applying processes and procedures.* Whilst critical thinking helps in effective decision making, it is not merely a set of procedures to be followed in order to resolve a practical problem or to judge which of a number of sources is the most credible.

- *Critical thinking is not aesthetic appreciation.* Some disciplines use the term 'critical thinking' to mean critical or aesthetic *appreciation*, for example textual analysis or commentary on a text as demanded in an English language or literature task. This might involve the application of critical thinking skills to construct a reasoned argument (which will be discussed in Chapter 7), but aesthetic or literary appreciation in itself does not constitute critical thinking.
- *Critical thinking is not creative thinking.* Underlying much of the work on creative thinking is the idea that creative thinking declines as childhood passes, or is undermined by education, and that creativity and creative thinking are the antithesis of reasoning. Creativity is seen as intelligent problem solving, innovative on the part of the originator or within its particular field. (In other words, creativity is producing something for the first time that you did not know had already been produced elsewhere.) Some courses in creative thinking provide training in brainstorming and concept-mapping techniques, but neither of these is critical thinking (although they are thinking skills that can be used to underpin the higher-level activities of analysing, evaluating and synthesising or creating, as seen in Bloom's Revised Taxonomy (see Chapter 2, page 48).
- *Critical thinking is not verbal reasoning.* Ability in critical thinking assessments is likely to correlate with success in verbal reasoning tests because the verbal reasoning questions assess ability to understand and manipulate information expressed in words. Verbal reasoning requires the ability to make logical decisions and to spot when insufficient data has been provided for a definitive conclusion to be reached. Verbal reasoning is, therefore, a thinking skill, but is not the same as critical thinking. Verbal reasoning tests (sometimes called psychometric tests or – confusingly – critical reasoning tests) are popular with employers and graduate recruiters as a tool for selecting managers and professional employees.
- *Critical thinking is not lateral thinking.* Edward de Bono coined the term 'lateral thinking', and argues that traditional, logical (or 'vertical') thinking can inhibit creative thinking and problem solving. He propounds the use of 'thinking tools' to improve the quality of thinking and arrive at solutions from unorthodox angles (De Bono, 1967 and subsequent publications). De Bono's course 'Six Thinking Hats' has been used by many organisations to develop creative rather than critical thinking. De Bono also

popularised the term 'parallel thinking', which he advocates as an alternative to 'the traditional argument or adversarial thinking [of Socrates, Plato and Aristotle, where] each side takes a different position and then seeks to attack the other side' (although in doing so they would not be applying the principle of charity outlined above). In parallel thinking, solutions generated by brainstorming should be considered alongside each other. Again, these approaches involve thinking skills, and could be usefully integrated in a thinking and reasoning skills course, but they are not necessarily critical thinking, which De Bono appears to rather disapprove of. Critical thinking generally concentrates on the rational in the everyday rather than other forms of thinking.

- *Critical thinking is not formal logic.* At the other extreme, critical thinking is sometimes confused with formal logic. Formal logic, like critical thinking, has its roots in philosophy and offers a method of assessing argument, but formal logic differs in that it focuses on assessing reasoning based on whether or not it is logically valid. This is a fairly typical example of what you might encounter in the early stages of a course in formal logic:

> All grizzlewigs can cook.
> Ivan is a grizzlewig.
> Therefore Ivan can cook.

The argument is logically valid but complete nonsense. The grizzlewigs do not exist.

Critical thinking was a response to the inadequacy of formal logic for analysing and evaluating real-life issues using normal human communication. Unlike formal logic, the critical thinking approach is to consider the factual and other content of communication and reasoning as well as any argument it contains. Some practitioners prefer the term *informal logic* rather than critical thinking. Familiarity with formal logic can be useful, and provide shortcuts, if you are preparing to teach critical thinking, but it is not essential. In some instances it has been found to hinder rather than help, since real human communication tends to be sloppier than formal logic allows. Attempts to force informal, everyday reasoning into the straitjacket of formal logic are, therefore, often counterproductive rather than helpful.

- *Critical thinking is not the new general studies.* Teachers may also need to respond to perceptions that critical thinking is simply a new label for general studies. It is not. In general studies courses, knowledge and skills from a range of disciplines (usually sciences, humanities and social sciences) are studied in an integrated way to develop an appreciation of how they relate to one another and how each may contribute to the understanding of issues being studied. General studies courses often have aims that overlap with those of critical thinking courses: examining issues from a range of perspectives, thinking logically and creatively, assessing the relative merits of evidence, making informed judgements, using arguments, and reaching justifiable conclusions. Thinking skills can be taught successfully through general studies, by using opportunities to draw distinctions between knowledge, truth and belief, and to recognise common fallacies, deductive and inductive arguments, and arguments from analogy, cause and authority, but this does not make critical thinking and general studies the same discipline.

Snapshots of critical thinking approaches in different education systems

Until the last decade, work in the field of thinking skills and critical thinking was concentrated in schools and universities within the USA, but there is important expertise in a number of other countries, where major thinking skills or critical thinking programmes have been incorporated in the school curricula. The brief descriptions given below of different approaches offer starting points for delivery models.

Australia

In common with many other industrialised countries, Australian Government policy is that teachers in all areas of education should develop their students' thinking skills. Many Australian universities run courses in critical thinking at undergraduate level and thinking skills are integrated into the school curriculum. The Australian Council for Educational Research (ACER) runs a number of critical thinking tests on behalf of Australian universities. Some of these tests are generic, but others are designed to test critical thinking within a discipline. ACER also offers a critical thinking test for employers to use in assessing people for appointment or promotion. ACER has suggested that higher-order thinking skills can be assessed in three ways: 'digging down' through the curriculum, 'looking beyond' the curriculum, and 'exploring under' the curriculum. However, the tests it offers currently assess reasoning and critical thinking through multiple choice tests.

Work on critical thinking in Australia has been significantly influenced by cognitive science research. Tim van Gelder contends that expertise in critical thinking is acquired only through a great deal of 'deliberate practice'. Van Gelder's work emphasises the use of argument maps – diagrams showing argument structure – and suggests that, to be effective, the practice should be deliberate, scaffolded, graduated and incorporating sufficient feedback. His approach has focused on the development of software packages for argument mapping and a number of such products have been successfully marketed through his commercial arm, Austhink, which offers packages designed for particular applications, including business decision making (Van Gelder et al., 2004).

Canada

There is no central federal control of education in Canada. Some territories deliver well-tried critical thinking programmes. The approach of Canadian schools typically embeds critical thinking into the school curriculum rather than seeing it as an add-on or discrete subject. Quebec, for example, possibly reflecting French influence on its educational system, very positively encourages the teaching of critical thinking: 'Schools have an important role to play in developing students' critical faculties, by teaching them to weigh all the facts, to take into consideration their own emotions, to use logical arguments, to take the context into account, to allow for ambiguity and to weed out preconceptions' (Government of Quebec, 2001, p. 20).

The Critical Thinking Consortium (TC²) in Vancouver has made a significant contribution to teaching of the subject in Canadian schools. Before TC² was formed in 1993, a Ministry (of British Columbia) report had noted, 'no single accepted definition of critical thinking [is] currently in use in British Columbia' – which was much the case elsewhere. TC² advocates embedding critical thinking within the curriculum rather than seeing it as an add-on or set of generic skills to be developed separately from content. The TC² model uses critical thinking vocabulary (e.g. inference, observation, generalisation, premise, conclusion, bias and point of view), and stresses critical thinking dispositions. TC² offers a wide range of resources to support critical thinking with primary and secondary classes in various subject areas, mainly humanities. (See www.tc2.ca.)

Canadian university scholarship in the field of critical thinking flourishes. Particularly worth mentioning is the work of Trudy Govier in synthesising critical thinking, ethical reasoning and conflict resolution.

Singapore

Singapore's Government has placed thinking skills and critical thinking at the heart of the education system, which has been singled out for scrutiny by governments aiming to emulate Singapore's economic success. The 'Thinking Schools, Learning Nation' (TSLN) vision was launched in 1997, with the aim of developing students' creative thinking skills, lifelong learning and, interestingly, nationalistic commitment. The former prime minister, Goh Chok Tong, promoted the concept of 'thinking schools', which would nurture thinking and committed citizens, able to sustain Singapore's position in the global economy.

More recently, Singapore's 'Junior College' curriculum has been revised to promote critical thinking and other skills. In 2006, in collaboration with Cambridge International Examinations, Singapore introduced a new GCE A Level subject, Knowledge and Inquiry (KI), which explores the nature of information and knowledge, and different methods of inquiry in the sciences, humanities, mathematics and the aesthetics. It incorporates training in critical thinking, including presenting cogent arguments (Tan, 2006).

United Kingdom

Until relatively recently, UK interest in critical thinking was primarily within higher education institutions. During the 1990s, the work of both Alec Fisher and Anne Thomson at the University of East Anglia's Centre for Research in Critical Thinking, together with the examination board Cambridge Assessment, contributed to the introduction of critical thinking into the school curriculum and its assessment. Although this centre has since disappeared without a trace, courses designed specifically to develop students' critical thinking capacities have been introduced within the 16–19 phase of secondary education, often as a result of initiatives by individual enthusiasts.

England and Wales

Changes to the National Curriculum for England, with effect from 2008, aimed to bring greater coherence to pre-16 pupils' learning experience through a set of unifying curriculum 'dimensions', which include 'sustainable futures and the global dimension' and 'creativity and critical thinking'. Schools should develop their students' thinking skills and critical thinking, within the personal, learning and thinking skills (PLTS) framework. The PLTS framework comprises six groups, intended to turn pupils into independent enquirers, creative thinkers, reflective learners, team workers, self-managers and effective participants.

In a development unrelated to the National Curriculum changes, between 1998 and 2007 there was a remarkable growth in critical thinking as an examination subject offered to post-16 students in England and Wales – remarkable in the light of the shortage of trained subject teachers and the absence of any supporting government initiative. This expansion can be explained partly by factors that have little to do with the merits of the subject. It would be unkind to suggest that curriculum managers make decisions with a view to maximising funding or improving their institution's league table position, but schools undoubtedly spotted the potential of critical thinking as a 'quick win' examination subject – especially since it not only provided curriculum breadth, but there was also a perception that it could be taught in less than a full timetable slot.

Scotland

Critical thinking is available to students in Scotland in the form of a unit which contributes to a National Qualification at Higher level.

USA

Thinking skills and critical thinking have a longer history in the USA than elsewhere, and, as has been seen in this chapter, US universities have dominated work in this discipline. Schools routinely teach critical thinking, and university applicants are required to sit the Scholastic Assessment Test (SAT), which assesses a number of aspects of academic aptitude, including critical thinking.

It is probable that thinking skills will assume even greater importance in the near future. In October 2009, Barack Obama said: 'The solution to low test scores is not lower standards; it's tougher, clearer standards … I'm calling on our nation's governors and state education chiefs to develop standards and assessments [that measure] 21st century skills like problem-solving and critical thinking.'[9]

Why introduce critical thinking?

We have outlined the development of the thinking skills approaches, and introduced key research and approaches taken in some countries. The impetus for the introduction of thinking skills or critical thinking may originate in government policy or in decisions taken at institution-level. However, if you have set up a thinking skills or critical thinking course, its success will hinge, above all, on the institution's commitment and your own, which in turn will depend on an appreciation of the benefits for students. Those benefits will be considered in the next section.

The critically thinking reader is likely to have spotted that the writers of this book have a vested interest in arguing that students will benefit from courses teaching thinking skills and critical thinking. The perceived benefits for critical thinking are usually seen in terms of personal development, intellectual growth and academic achievement. Does the available evidence support these claims? In the UK, most evaluations to date of the impact on learners of thinking skills programmes have focused on generic thinking skills rather than critical thinking. Thinking skills interventions have generally been relatively small-scale projects, and the sample scrutinised insufficient to enable reliable conclusions to be drawn about the potential impact of larger-scale interventions.

Evaluation of any innovation in classroom practice is not necessarily conclusive: even if there is a control group, it is not possible to be sure that student progress is the result of the innovation or simply of the increased maturity of the learners. Furthermore, taking part in any initiative appears to bring for learners positive effects that are not sustained when the programme is introduced more widely. It has been suggested that the positive effects may have as much to do with the enthusiasm and drive that innovators bring as with the content of the actual project. Certainly the authors' experience has been that enthusiasm on the part of the teacher is essential to a successful critical thinking course.

Benefits for students from the study of critical thinking

Critical thinking helps develop independent, thinking individuals with desirable intellectual and personality traits

There have been numerous attempts to identify the intellectual and personality traits that are developed through a critical thinking course. Typical lists of the characteristics of critical thinkers include qualities such as:

- being interested in other people's ideas, but intellectually independent, and prepared to reassess their own ideas and beliefs in the face of sound evidence and argument;
- ability to recognise their own weaknesses, and accepting responsibility;
- willingness to question, but resistance to manipulation;
- ability to synthesise and find connections between subjects;
- ability to base conclusions on sound arguments.

Not surprisingly, non-critical thinkers demonstrate the converse of these traits. For example, as human beings we tend to see connections, often where none exist. ('I had the worst dose of flu ever five days after I had the flu vaccination, so the vaccination must have caused it.') We also tend to accept evidence that supports our opinions, behaviour or actions, and ignore or reject evidence that does not. ('Chocolate is good for anaemia.' 'A glass of red wine helps prevent cardio-vascular problems.') Even if we do not believe that crystal dangling or white energy waves can cure our bad back, most of us still hold on to some attitudes that are ingrained by our upbringing ('You must always wear clean underwear, in case you are knocked down by a bus and taken to hospital'), rather than supported by evidence. Training in critical thinking does not completely eliminate irrationality, but it provides tools for discriminating between the vast amounts of information presented by global media and through the internet.

Critical thinking is useful preparation for decision making in life

Critical thinking gives students techniques for making judgements, because it develops their abilities to consider different perspectives on issues, to assess reasons and evidence, and to make choices from alternatives based on sound reasoning. It also gives students tools for judging the credibility of any person or source that offers advice or information, as well as tools for evaluating that advice. Critical thinking skills empower.

Studying critical thinking underpins students' wider studies and enhances their achievement in other subjects

There is some evidence that encouraging learners' generic thinking skills helps their achievement in other subjects. UK schools which introduced critical thinking as a separate subject for post-16 students reported that students' essay-writing skills improved and their performance in other examination subjects was enhanced. Evidence for this at present is both anecdotal and supported by research (Black, 2008). For example, according to *The Times*, Colyton Grammar School students achieved the 'best A-level results in England' in 2004 and 2005. The head teacher ascribed this success to the fact that all students were prepared for GCE Advanced Subsidiary Critical Thinking in addition to their chosen Advanced Level subjects, and thereby gained a better insight into their other subjects (Halpin, 2005). A year later, Colyton repeated their achievement and the head teacher stated, 'In grade terms, its contribution is relatively modest, but we are absolutely convinced that it contributes to their performance at A level by encouraging them to be more analytical in their approach' (Halpin and Blair, 2006).

Critical thinking is a key academic competency, which higher education prizes

Performance in standard tests of critical thinking ability (SATS) is a key selection criterion used by US universities. UK medical, veterinary and law schools, and recruiting universities such as Cambridge, use thinking skills assessments to differentiate among a superfluity of highly qualified applicants. (Chapter 8 provides an overview of these assessments.)

Universities aim not only to recruit applicants with critical thinking skills, but also to develop these skills in their own students. Studying critical thinking enhances achievement in pre-university students, and success in higher education correlates to critical thinking skills. Professor Tim Birkhead of Sheffield University has written:

> A large proportion of university assessments rely on undergraduates preparing coherent, unambiguous written accounts of experiments, field course exercises, research projects or reviews of the literature. Professional scientists, and those who teach undergraduates, have to be able to write … and clear writing still means clear thinking …
>
> With the right guidance and motivation, writing can be mastered. A more serious obstacle facing new undergraduates (and sometimes old ones, too) is thinking for themselves. Not in terms of day-to-day survival, but intellectually.
>
> I recently suggested elsewhere that an A-level in 'thinking for myself' ought to be a requirement for university entrance, at least in some disciplines. No such A-level exists, but I was surprised to learn that one called critical thinking does … Wondering whether this might be little more than airy-fairy twaddle, I obtained the latest specifications and a selection of textbooks, and was duly impressed.
>
> It is reassuring that some schools already offer the critical thinking AS/A-level. A qualification in that subject, alongside regular A-levels, would be a huge bonus and would go some way towards making the transition between school and university more satisfying all round. (Birkhead, 2009)

Critical thinking is a key competency for economic survival in the twenty-first-century global economy and, as a result, governments and policy-makers expect education to develop learners' critical thinking

The snapshots of thinking skills in different countries give some indication of the importance that is placed on the development of students' thinking skills and critical thinking. The global economy, the pace of technological change and the impact of information and communication technology have meant that the ability to handle and to adapt information is essential to enable individuals and societies to meet the resulting challenges. Numerous governments and transnational organisations, including the USA, Australia, Hong Kong, the countries of the UK and the European Union, have established similar lists of key competencies for life and work in twenty-first-century society. The EU groups critical thinking with 'underpinning transversal competences', such as creativity, initiative, problem solving, risk assessment, decision taking and constructive management of feelings. These key competencies are regarded as essential to the individual's employability in a rapidly changing global economy. Put simply, employers want employees who can think through problems logically and be adaptable.

On the one hand, governments and their policy-makers are promoting educational approaches that foster critical thinking, because they expect education to have as its goal the development of people who can contribute to the economic well-being of their country and participate fully as citizens in a democratic society. On the other hand, teachers want their students to acquire the capacity for critical thought so that they will question and evaluate the messages they receive from news media, advertising and government bodies. Either way, critical thinking skills benefit the individual.

The savvy user of digital technologies and media is a critical thinker

Digital literacy (or information literacy) involves 'confident and critical use of electronic media for work, leisure and communication' and is related to critical thinking, information management skills, and communication skills (European Commission Directorate-General for Education and Culture, 2004). Critical thinking skills help the user of digital technologies to treat information with scepticism, evaluate sources of information, discriminate between evidence and opinion, and decide for themselves what to believe and do. When there is a surfeit of information, critical thinking skills enable the user to differentiate between plausible, useful, irrelevant and suspect 'facts'.

Critical thinking is enjoyable

Well, the authors would say that, wouldn't they? But compared with other subjects, critical thinking offers definite bonuses for students:

- the critical thinking content (the language of argument) can be learnt comparatively quickly;
- students can select their own subject content in terms of the topics through which the skills are developed;
- homework can be kept to a minimum;
- most students enjoy discussion and argument (in the everyday sense) and critical thinking lessons should provide plenty of opportunity for this;
- subject to the demands of any examination syllabus, the course can cover topics which tap into students' own interests. You will not need any excuse for bringing trashy newspapers into the classroom or for studying conspiracy theories.

7   Integrating the Skills

'Thinking is hard work.'

Promenades philosophiques (1905–09), Remy de Gourmont
(1858–1915)

Once the decision has been made that the curriculum should include a programme designed to develop students' thinking and reasoning skills, or specifically critical thinking, there are a number of issues to be considered to ensure successful implementation. The questions which teachers most often ask at the planning stage are addressed in Chapter 9 (see the online resources available at http://education.matthewslally.continuumbooks. com). This chapter considers the specific issue of whether thinking and reasoning skills should be delivered discretely or integrated within teaching of other subjects. Strategies for the latter are outlined and some sample activities provided. Within the scope of this book it is possible to discuss only a limited number of subjects, but the strategies outlined can be adapted for use in other subjects.

Should Thinking Skills and Critical Thinking be Taught Discretely or be Infused or Integrated within Other Subjects?

There is no simple answer to this. Indeed different researchers have at different times made the case for a range of approaches, which will be discussed below. (The critical thinker may wonder whether the perceived success of a chosen approach is due not so much to the merit of the approach but rather to the enthusiasm and additional effort which a classroom initiative generates.) In common with other skill areas (e.g. vocational, basic employability and functional skills), thinking skills programmes tend to fall into one of three categories:

- targeting thinking skills in isolation as a *discrete* programme of study;

- *infusing* thinking skills in a generic way across all subjects and lessons;
- exploring thinking skills by *integrating* them within a specific subject.

In addition to these three models for teaching thinking skills, other approaches fall somewhere between different models. The challenge for institutions is to determine which model will be most effective with their own students. Any process of selecting or designing a suitable model needs to take into account the available resources and expertise, timetable constraints, and whether or not students will attempt external examinations.

Targeting generic thinking skills in isolation as a discrete programme of study

The generic thinking skills are usually considered to be problem solving, creativity, decision making and critical thinking (but not necessarily in the sense of skill in handling reasoned argument). There are various programmes available that focus on developing students' metacognition, or thinking about their own thinking, and that target wider thinking skills discretely. These programmes include Feuerstein's Instrumental Enrichment; the similar Somerset Thinking Skills programme developed by Nigel Blagg (Blagg, Ballinger and Gardner, 2003); and Edward de Bono's creative thinking programme 'Six Thinking Hats'. The expectation is that students will subsequently be able to apply the skills developed during the course when they study other disciplines or subjects. Dramatic successes have been claimed for some of these programmes – a TES headline in 1996 concerning Professor Feuerstein's work with children with learning difficulties, described him as 'The man who can work wonders, (TES, 12 April 1996).

Courses leading to a test or qualification in critical thinking (skill in handling reasoned argument) or problem solving normally fall within the category of programmes that teach thinking skills discretely, because they target the thinking skills separately from specialist subject knowledge.

For institutions and teachers, the issue is whether or not 'pure' thinking skills can be taught discretely and then applied to other situations/subjects, or whether they can be taught only within a subject discipline, as argued by McPeck (McPeck, 1981). McPeck's position is explored below in the context of integration approaches. However, the evidence from critical thinking teachers is that students trained as critical thinkers using general material can reason better in their specialist subjects than those untrained in critical thinking. Models that develop domain-specific thinking through the curriculum have been classified as either 'infusion' or 'integration' approaches.

Infusing thinking skills in a generic way across all lessons

Infusion approaches embed thinking skills within the teaching of the wider curriculum. They are often seen as more suitable for primary schools, where children spend most of the time with one class teacher who normally takes responsibility for the full curriculum for that class. However, infusion approaches have been successfully adopted by teachers working in subject areas at post-primary level. Typically, generic thinking skills are infused directly with topics or cross-subject themes, with the dual aims of deepening understanding of content and enhancing critical thinking (in the wider sense). Infusion approaches identify contexts where particular thinking skills can be developed; for example, causal reasoning in a science lesson, decision-making strategies applied to personal life, and hypothesising about fictional or historical characters. The benefits claimed for the infusion approach are that transfer and reinforcement of learning are facilitated.

Typical infusion approaches include communities of enquiry, such as those promoted by the philosophy for children movement and epitomised in the work of the Society for Advancing Philosophical Enquiry and Reflection in Education (SAPERE). The 'community of enquiry' involves establishing a classroom climate conducive to critical reflection. The contention is that when an appropriate classroom environment is established, 'philosophical enquiry' takes place through classroom discussion, which encourages the use of thinking skills and reasoned analysis. 'Thinking' is defined as having various components (creative thinking, critical thinking and problem solving).

Robert Fisher is a leading exponent of thinking skills programmes for primary schools. Fisher built on Lipman's Philosophy for Children model (Lipman, Sharp, and Oscanyan, 2003). The processes defined in Fisher's work support the current emphasis on learning outcomes, inquiry learning, cooperative group work and the development of the individual by encouraging questioning and the exploration of questions that arise in classroom interaction. Activating Children's Thinking Skills (ACTS) in Northern Ireland and the Critical Thinking Consortium (TC²) in Vancouver have both developed similar programmes.

Exploring thinking skills by integrating them within a specific subject

Integration approaches are very similar to infusion approaches. If there is a difference, it is that infusion can be operated when the curriculum is not broken into separate subjects, and integration applies when students are taught subjects separately by specialist teachers. In the integration model, thinking skills are incorporated within a specific subject and discipline-specific thinking skills are taught, e.g. mathematical thinking.

Commentators such as McPeck have argued strongly against the teaching of thinking skills or critical thinking as separate subjects and claimed that they cannot exist outside a subject discipline or domain (McPeck, 1981). Scientific thinking is an example of domain-specific thinking. Proponents of this approach argue that good thinking is underpinned by the concept structures and methods of the specific subject. When reasoning outside that subject domain, thinking is less effective because the concept structures are not present. It is, however, entirely possible (and supported by evidence) that the trained critical thinker would still reason better in any situation – or discipline – than an untrained thinker.

Integration approaches are exemplified in the work on geography teaching carried out by David Leat and other researchers at Newcastle University (Leat, 1998). The Cognitive Acceleration through Science Education (CASE) programme developed at the King's College London (Adey, Shayer and Yates, 1995) and Cognitive Acceleration through Mathematics Education (CAME) are other examples.

Strategies for integrating thinking skills and critical thinking within other subjects

At the start of the course it is important that you establish what the main aim is, and that you make it clear to students, so they will buy into it.

- *'Critical thinking light'*: The subject discipline is the main (or sole) examination target, and, in order to enhance students' achievement it is taught through a thinking skills approach, including some critical thinking skills. In this scenario, the scheme of work needs to be built around the subject syllabus, and the subject content taught through activities that implicitly develop thinking skills. An example of this model would be religious studies with critical thinking.
- *Curriculum enrichment with critical thinking*: The two subjects (the enrichment subject and critical thinking) are equally weighted in terms of the examinations that students will (or perhaps will not) take. Citizenship studies or general studies with critical thinking are examples of this model. This approach is more likely to be successful if the key critical thinking content is taught explicitly early on in the course, so the skills can then be practised through subject topics. The CIE Global Perspectives Course, for

example, explicitly assesses thinking and reasoning skills through the global perspectives content.

Encouraging a questioning mindset

(In this section, problem solving has its wider meaning and does not refer exclusively to the type of data handling and modelling questions often tested through multiple choice questions.)

The tools for teaching that have been described in Chapters 2, 3, 4 and 5 provide guidance on embedding thinking and reasoning skills within teaching, and are equally relevant for integrating thinking skills within other subjects. Integrating activities that stimulate critical thinking (rather than just knowledge recall) into course teaching primarily means providing plenty of opportunities for exploration of the issues, problems and questions that crop up naturally – ideally those that arise out of students' own contributions.

When you start teaching a course that integrates critical thinking within another subject, there is no need to chuck out the subject-based resources that have worked in the past. Instead, adapt your existing teaching materials to focus on encouraging students to raise and deal with questions and problems within the context of the subject.

Encourage students to develop a questioning attitude by treating the questions they raise as worth exploring. Whenever they read a section of the textbook or an information sheet, students should write down the questions that occur to them as they read, however trivial those questions may appear. Students' own questions can then be used as the basis for class discussion, helped along with further questions such as:

- What do you think about this?
- What are your *reasons* for thinking that …? (This gives students practice in justifying their opinions by providing supporting reasons.)
- What does that imply? (This encourages them to draw conclusions.)
- What explains …?
- What would be the result of …?
- What if …? (This should lead to hypothetical reasoning.)

Problem solving within academic disciplines and subjects

Academic disciplines have their own types of problems and their own way of looking at problems. In the study of English literature, problems are about interpretation of literary texts; in science they are about formulating and testing a verifiable hypothesis; in business studies they are about decision making in a business environment often using realistic case studies.

Problem solving demands a complex combination of thinking and reasoning skills: critical thinking skills are applied to analyse the issue; creative thinking takes place when possible solutions are generated. A problem is simply a real or abstract situation that needs a solution. Let's say the problem is, 'We have to teach critical thinking.' We can rephrase this particular problem as an issue or a question, '*How* do we teach critical thinking?' More demanding problems usually include an element of conflict, which presents obstacles to a solution. Such problems (or issues) may challenge students' beliefs, preconceptions and biases, involve ethical issues, and require the consideration of alternative explanations.

Strategies for incorporating problem solving into the course

Developing students' problem-solving skills means presenting them with problems to be solved (or issues to be resolved if you prefer the alternative terminology).

- Build your own stash of suitable problems. Suitable problems are both mini-topics and the major questions the subject is concerned with.
- Start lessons with a mini-problem. Small groups develop alternative solutions expressed in a limited number of words, say maximum fifty. One student reads out the mini-solution to the whole class. The teacher and other groups can suggest a mini-counter-argument.
- Begin with manageable problems that reflect students' level of understanding and maturity. If you are teaching CIE's Pre-U Global Perspectives, you will need to find ways of making global issues manageable for your students. Global issues are not only remote from students' own experience, but can be overwhelming. 'How can the school cut its fuel use?' is more accessible than 'How should Western nations eliminate climate change?' You may find it beneficial to help students move from local to national to international problems, and finally to see the links between them.
- Successful problem-solving activities engage students' interest. Invite students to suggest problems and issues or, better still, allow problems to arise naturally out of the subject content you are teaching.
- The problem needs to be outlined clearly to students, including any necessary context, events, facts and participants. The problem

should give rise to a question or issue, which students will need to analyse.

- When the problem is expressed, it should not contain a value judgement (statement of what is right, wrong or useful based on personal opinion). This can be especially tricky where the subject is religious studies or ethics. A problem expressed with an implicit value judgement would be, 'How can the needless slaughter of unborn babies be stopped?' 'What should the Government do to help reduce teenage pregnancy?' would be preferable.
- Group work encourages the creative generation of solutions.
- Before selecting their preferred solution from the possibilities they have identified, students may need directing to use the specific skills of:

  a) examining evidence
  b) considering alternative viewpoints
  c) considering alternative solutions
  d) considering consequences of the possible solutions.

- If controversial topics, likely to provoke sensitive reactions, are to be tackled it is advisable to lay down ground rules:

  a) students must accept certain principles:
     1. that they should respect the right of others to hold differing views, even when disagreeing with those views;
     2. that the view is separated from the person;
     3. that they may be wrong;
     4. that they should clarify meaning when asked;
     5. and that they should give reasons for claims they make or beliefs they express.
  b) the person contributing opinions and information is treated with respect, however objectionable those opinions may be. (This aspiration could be difficult to enforce.)

- Make sure there are pauses for reflecting on and reviewing the way the group has worked together. This can help students develop another attribute of critical thinkers – conflict resolution skills.
- As well as opportunities for considering questions that arise in class discussion, written assignments should ask students to apply their thinking and reasoning skills by dealing with problems and issues, not simply to regurgitate information.

Problem-solving activities

General discussion

Problem solving differs from other reasoning activities in that it is based in a situation (real or abstract) that needs resolving, and the possible solution is reached by examining the situation, the evidence and the alternatives.

The two health care funding activities below show how problem solving can be introduced. The first activity can develop thinking and reasoning skills, since it requires students to construct their own and challenge others' arguments, identify principles, and apply (ethical) principles. This activity could be improved, and made more authentic, by the inclusion of an article or information about a genuine case. The second activity also provides opportunities for development of problem-solving skills because it asks students to research and examine evidence, consider alternatives, and finally to generate solutions.

Activity One – health care funding

£10,000 would provide a new and expensive course of a cancer treatment drug for one person. The health care provider has refused to fund the treatment because cheaper alternatives are available. Write a reasoned argument either for or against the money being spent on this treatment.

> **Comment**
> Reasons for paying for the above drug treatment could include: the treatment is more effective, has fewer side effects, and the drug is the last hope for some people. Governments spend money on things that are less beneficial (ask for examples). Health care should be provided at the point of need irrespective of ability to pay (a principle). Drug treatments are expensive to start with, while the costs of development are recouped; then they become cheaper.
> Reasons offered against funding could include: money is limited, cheaper treatments exist, and new treatments are untried and unproven.

Activity Two – health care funding

Students answer the questions below.

1. List what you think are the five most common causes of death in young people aged 17–25.
2. Research the causes of death in the population as a whole and among young people. Find the *actual* five most common causes

of death in both groups. (Don't forget to state the age ranges of both groups.)

3. A budget of £10,000 is available for your local health centre to spend on health care for young people. Prepare a reasoned case recommending how the money should be spent. Your answer should:

   b) outline the options available;
   c) explain the possible benefits and disadvantages of each option;
   d) identify the evidence which supports your recommended option.

Strategies for developing students' writing skills within the discipline

Writing, thinking and reasoning are inseparable. If students reach university, they will be expected to demonstrate critical thinking whenever they write academic essays or reports within their chosen discipline. Assignments that require drafting and redrafting help focus thinking and sharpen thinking and reasoning within the subject. When students write a traditional humanities essay they tend to try to show the teacher (or examiner) that they can produce a convincing essay. This is not necessarily the same as actually presenting a convincing argument to support a claim or point of view, although good essays incorporate structure and reasoning. The ability to present an argument will improve students' essay-writing. Setting tasks that require students to formulate and justify a point of view helps them develop and present their own arguments.

Developing students' critical thinking through writing does not mean you will be setting (and marking) endless essays or reports. It can be done equally well through plenty of short writing tasks. Writing a brief written response challenges students to sharpen their thinking, because they have to be selective with reasons and argument structure. Producing letters, reviews, and presentations can all help students understand the differences between persuasive argument, rhetoric, explanation, etc.

Activities to develop students' thinking through writing

Building a subject-focused critical thinking portfolio
Students build their own portfolio of phrases and arguments (their own and other people's) within the *context of the subject*. They use their file to help write counter-examples or counter-arguments. The file could

include phrases and argument indicators printed out onto card and used to construct arguments at different stages of the course.

When they have developed confidence, students (especially if they are preparing for CIE Global Perspectives) can use presentation software, or the interactive whiteboard, to present their own short argument to the group.

Summary writing

Students write a summary (150 or 200 words) of an article or textbook chapter that presents an opinion or viewpoint on an issue. Then students swap summaries and do *one* of the following:

- summarise the summary (100 words) for someone who knows nothing about the subject;
- write a short, reasoned case (100 words) that provides a persuasive argument in favour of the views in the first summary;
- write a short reasoned case (100 words) that counters the views in the first summary;
- expand the first summary by adding reasons, evidence or examples to support the viewpoint given.

Round robin reasoning

This activity is suited to humanities essays or science tasks, which provide the opportunity for the answer to be presented as a reasoned argument. All questions should test the syllabus content. This activity enables students to:

- develop their subject knowledge;
- practise answering exam-style questions;
- enhance their skills in assessing argument;
- practise writing their own arguments;
- experience collaborative working and peer review, both of which they will meet in higher education or in future employment.

All students carry out the roles of both *Student 1* and *Reviewer 1*. They can be organised as one or more 'round robins'. If preferred, work can be passed from one student to another anonymously, but you will need a tracking system to ensure you know who has produced what.

1. As *Student 1*, every student receives a different question and produces a first draft answer in the form of an argument. (It will help the reviewer if the answer is printed out with a wide margin or on the left-hand half of the page only.)
2. All students' first draft answers are collected in and date-marked.

3. Each first draft is passed to a different student, *Reviewer 1*, who

   - responds to the argument either by producing a counter-argument or evaluating *Student 1*'s argument – students will need clear instructions as to what is wanted;
   - comments on how *Student 1*'s draft answer could be improved;
   - produces their own version of how they think the question should be answered.

4. *Student 1* uses *Reviewer 1*'s comments to produce their second (final) draft, which is then submitted for marking.

5. At the end of the process all students have submitted four pieces of work:

   - a first draft answer to a question;
   - a second (final) draft answer to the same question;
   - comments on another student's response to a different question;
   - their own answer to that question.

6. This whole process can be repeated again with a third student as *Reviewer 2* reviewing *Student 1*'s work and producing an answer to the question.

Presentations by outside speakers

Arranging a series of guest speakers can add an additional dimension to any course that targets thinking and reasoning skills, particularly so if students are being prepared for CIE Global Perspectives. One or two speakers per term can be invited to give short presentations (maximum 30 minutes) on a range of topics. Topics should relate to the course, but not necessarily form part of the core syllabus, and should stimulate different perspectives and opinions. Students could suggest organisations and topics to provide the springboard for further activities e.g.:

- local branch of national campaigning organisations such as Amnesty International, Shelter, Greenpeace, or *The Big Issue* to speak on government policy affecting their area of concern;
- local business (e.g. bank, environmental services company) to speak on an ethical business issue;
- an academic from a local higher education institution – political or economic topics;
- local historical society – arguing for preservation of, or funding for, renovation of a building of interest;

- local councillor – in favour of, or against, a proposed or recent council initiative (e.g. local shopping centre redevelopment, demolishing homes to build a new road, open-cast coal-mining, quarrying, etc.);
- local trade unionist – the work of trade unions historically and today.

Activities linked to a presentation by an outside speaker

1. Students research an aspect of the topic of presentation beforehand. This could include the work of the speaker's organisation or background information about the speaker.
2. The invited speaker should be briefed beforehand, so it is understood that a persuasive presentation leading to a clear conclusion is wanted, and warned that students have been encouraged to exercise their argument skills.
3. The speaker gives a short presentation (maximum 30 minutes) followed by an opportunity for students to ask questions.
4. In small groups, students spend 15 to 20 minutes identifying the key points and perspectives raised by the speaker.
5. Students write a review (not a summary) and evaluation of the speaker's presentation. This task can be carried out in twos or threes. The review should be short – maximum 350 words – to encourage structured rather than discursive writing. Students' reviews could include:

   - brief context about the speaker and the subject;
   - the main points of the speaker's presentation and the conclusion (either stated by the speaker or inferred – but be prepared for students to give different interpretations of what the speaker's conclusion was);
   - an alternative perspective on the issue, or a counter-argument;
   - the students' alternative conclusion supported by reasons.

Activities for students to do outside the classroom

- Students find and bring to the class a short article, letter to a newspaper or comment posted on a website, which relates to the subject and demonstrates some attempt at reasoning, but not necessarily a strong argument.
- Activities requiring students to research a topic work well. The topic should ideally be one that interests them, and that has been negotiated with the teacher. This type of task can be adapted at

different stages of the course. In a science course, students could find an article on a pseudo-scientific matter; for example, crop circles produced by aliens, sightings of UFOs, the efficacy of crystal dangling, etc. Students assess the credibility of sources and apply their reasoning skills to reach a view as to what most likely happened. In class, they present their research and conclusions to the group.

- An intranet can be used to create a subject e-community or online discussion group. Set some ground rules: offensive material, rants and irrelevant comments are vetoed, and students' contributions must relate to the subject and show some evidence of reasoning. Post articles or topics that will stimulate discussion.
- Other tried and tested activities are: subject-related journal reading (with a set task) and quizzes; reflection – students go away from the class thinking; planning for an activity that will take place in the next lesson; explicit exercise practice/worksheets ... and the usual written homework.

Integrating Critical Thinking in the Teaching of Specific Subjects

English literature

Syllabuses and textbooks for post-16 and undergraduate English literature courses introduce the discipline of advanced literary study and often claim to develop their capacity for 'critical analysis', 'critical theory' or sometimes 'critical thinking'. If you have reached this chapter of this book, you should be aware that 'critical analysis' and 'critical thinking' mean different things in different subjects. The focus in both English literature and critical thinking on the analysis of textual material sometimes misleads schools and literature teachers into assuming that the skills developed in a literature course will suffice to prepare students for a critical thinking examination. In short, they won't. (See Chapter 6 for what critical thinking isn't.)

If literature has a purpose, it is usually explained as giving meaning to our lives in that it attempts to come to terms with the complexities and disorder of human existence. The writer of a novel, play or poem presents an interpretation of human experience. Students should be applying reasoning strategies when they study literary texts, but these are different strategies to those used in studying non-literary texts, whether the non-literary material is simply information-giving, or is persuasive argument.

Critical thinking involves analysis, evaluation and development of argument (the attempt to persuade the reader to accept something). The critical thinker tries to get from the text the sense of what the author is saying (identifying the conclusion of the argument) and assess the strengths and weaknesses of the argument by identifying reasons, assumptions and evidence. The critical thinker also develops and presents reasoning.

Suppose we start with two students: the critical thinking student, faced with a passage containing argument, and the literature student, faced with an extract or poem to analyse. Our two students are both looking for meaning within the text, but should be engaging with their respective texts in different ways. Further, there are key differences between the types of texts they are likely to encounter.

Our two students approach the text attempting to answer key questions:
What is the text about?
What is the writer trying to say?

The critical thinking student should:

- decide whether or not there is an argument within the passage, by identifying the conclusion (if any) and the author's supporting reasons and evidence;
- assess the strength or otherwise of the passage *as a piece of reasoning.*

The literature student should:

- work out how the text works linguistically and emotionally;
- assess the writer's techniques, e.g. structure, content, use of language, metaphor, imagery;
- engage with the text to answer the question: '*What effect does the text have?*'

In critical thinking, texts:

- contain *reasoning*;
- *explicitly* convey an argument;
- have *implicit* meaning in terms of assumptions, inferences, underlying beliefs.

In the study of literature, texts:

- contain *meaning*, which may be conveyed *explicitly* and/or *implicitly*.

If we can find meaning – something that the writer is saying – within a literary text, it may be tempting to try to apply critical thinking techniques and consider whether the writer's meaning is supported.

This can work fairly obviously with certain texts. For example, the writer's message – the ghastliness of war, suffering, pity – is very apparent in First World War poems such as Siegfried Sassoon's 'Does it Matter?', Isaac Rosenberg's 'Break of Day in the Trenches', Wilfred Owen's 'Disabled' and 'Dulce et Decorum est'. The stumbling block to this type of approach is that literary texts have several layers of meaning – explicit and implicit. For example, Shakespeare's Sonnet 130 'My mistress' eyes are nothing like the sun' can be read explicitly as a description of his mistress' disagreeable features. However, an alternative reading (of love, albeit expressed humorously) can be drawn from the text. The reader can select the reading they prefer, and find other, implicit, meanings. Literature students tend to be more successful in essays and examinations if they avoid the temptation to argue that the author is presenting their viewpoint, or opinions about the world or society, through the text.

The other difficulty is that some literary texts can appear to be like argument because they are persuasive texts. You may indeed find that sections of text in a novel or play lend themselves to analysis and assessment as reasoning. However, the application of critical thinking techniques to finding meaning in a literary text is problematic: the reader needs to *engage with* the text to find meaning; alternative readings may be drawn from the text.

Applying critical thinking to the study of literature

As we have seen, teaching critical thinking through literature presents particular challenges, but this does not mean it will not work – just that you need to be clear about what you are trying to achieve. There are essentially two strands to the application of critical thinking to the study of literature:

- interpretation of the text: *critical analysis of literary text* uses *critical thinking skills* when the student engages with the text to arrive at their own interpretation of the text.
- presentation of one's own interpretation, which is achieved most successfully (in the eyes of examiners) when the student supports their interpretation with evidence (from the text, from other readings or critical opinions, or by applying a particular framework to interpreting the text, e.g. a feminist framework).

When integrating critical thinking into English literature, the teacher needs to ensure clarity of approach and not confuse *textual* analysis and interpretation with analysis and evaluation of *argument*. In practical terms, the teacher introduces the text to students and helps them form an individual, personal response to it. English literature examiners typically do not welcome examination scripts containing answers that appear to have been prepared, or excessively 'scaffolded'; for example, addressing content, style, imagery, sentence structure and so on, each in mind-numbing turn. Instead, examiners hope to read the student's genuine point of view (albeit rooted firmly in the text) on *what* is said together with *how* it is said. If this seems like an emotional response, contrasted with the requirements of the critical thinking examination, then it certainly is. The critical thinking student has opportunities to express and justify an opinion when they present their own argument on an issue raised in a text. It is, however, important for students to realise that answers based on an emotional response are unlikely to attract high marks in the critical thinking examination. At the same time, excessively scaffolded or pre-prepared work based on a formula or structure is generally frowned upon in critical thinking examinations. Originality of thought will be rewarded there if it is presented in the form of a sound, reasoned argument.

Bringing English literature and critical thinking together

The issues that arise when critical thinking is delivered through literature do not mean that the two subjects are incompatible: training students to be critical thinkers means helping them to deploy the right reasoning strategies in any situation, to compare their interpretations and reasoning with others', to revise or reject those interpretations, to support their reasoning with evidence and, not least, to value their own reasoning and opinions.

Activities to integrate critical thinking into literature

Critical thinking skills can be integrated into English literature in three main ways:

- Presenting their own interpretation of the text provides rich opportunities for students to generate and present arguments. Students can apply the techniques of creating effective reasoned argument when they write essays or contribute to class discussions. Class tasks, assignments and essays need to be constructed so that students become accustomed to giving reasons and evidence for the stance they are adopting.
- Opportunities are used to identify argument components and structure in extracts from literary or primary texts and critical commentaries.

- Literary texts very often present ethical and moral issues and dilemmas. Students can apply ethical reasoning strategies and hypothetical reasoning to exploration of those issues.

Issues in literature – as in other disciplines – are the questions that do not have one simple, obvious answer; in other words, the topics that literary critics dispute about. Students can use their critical thinking skills and incorporate reasoned argument in their assignments and essays only when they are answering questions that present a problem or issue for them to respond to.

Developing critical thinking through the study of literature means providing plenty of opportunities for students to present their own arguments through short pieces of writing, class discussion and essays. Students need to develop the self-assurance to move beyond looking for the 'right answer', which they hope the examiner will reward, and to be confident in presenting their own interpretations of the text. English literature examiners welcome originality of thought if it is grounded in the text. This can be encouraged by inviting students' initial impressions, raising questions, exploring possibilities, and providing opportunities for students to expound and defend their own interpretations. Questions for written answers and for discussion in class need to be worded on the lines of those given below to help develop students' specific critical thinking skills:

- 'What evidence is there for your claim?' (This asks students to support their opinions with reasons and evidence.)
- 'Clarify the meaning of the phrase "…"' or 'What do you mean by the word "…"?' (These encourage clarification of meaning and precision in communication.)
- 'What inferences can be made from the text?'
- 'What might the author have intended to express here?'
- (Where the text uses analogy) 'What is being compared here?' 'How effective is the analogy?'
- 'What is at issue here?' 'Does the text raise different perspectives?'
- 'To what extent (or how far) do you agree with the view that …?' 'Bloggs interprets this text as … Is her interpretation plausible?' (Students may need reminding of the meaning of 'plausible' (i.e. reasonable, not far-fetched)). 'What evidence is there for Bloggs' interpretation?'

When setting questions requiring written answers, direct students towards analysis and evaluations; e.g. 'Analyse the writer's choices of content, language and structure', or 'Evaluate the text in the light of critical theories or the opinions of literary authorities.'

Lesson Idea One: introducing critical thinking into the literature course

General discussion

When an English literature course is designed, there is potentially a vast choice of texts. In practice, the budget for new books is usually limited, so the suggested activities are based around a clutch of well-tried texts. It is intended that the activities are used as templates to be adapted for use with whatever text you happen to be teaching.

This lesson idea should ideally be based around a poem or extract required by the syllabus. One of the many First World War poems commonly studied would be suitable. The activity will:

- introduce students to the differences between critical thinking and critical appreciation of literature;
- help them to understand the difference between an argument (meaning a quarrel) and a reasoned argument;
- enable them to differentiate between argument and other types of text.

You will need a video clip of a quarrel and copies of the selected poem or extract.

Tasks

1 a) Begin by asking students for definitions of 'argument'. They are likely to start with argument as a quarrel.

 b) Show them a short video clip of a quarrel from a suitable text. (Suitable video clips include Elizabeth Bennett and Mr Darcy or Elizabeth Bennett and Lady Catherine de Bourgh (*Pride and Prejudice*), Montagues and Capulets (*Romeo and Juliet*), The Wife of Bath and Jankyn (Chaucer's *The Wife of Bath's Prologue and Tale*).

2 a) Give them the definition of argument in the critical thinking sense – an attempt to persuade the reader or listener to accept a claim, which the arguer supports with one or more reasons.

 b) Show a simple argument, such as the one below:

> *Reason:* Studying critical thinking through literature will help you think logically.
> *Reason:* It will also refine your aesthetic sensibilities.
> *Conclusion:* Therefore, you will be able to write better literature essays.

(If students disagree with this, all well and good. They can present their objections in the form of reasons and a conclusion.)

c) Point out the argument indicator word (therefore), and explain that other common words (because, so) often indicate that argument elements are present.

3. Discuss with students the types of reasoning used by the characters in the quarrel, and the strengths or weaknesses of that reasoning. (The questions suggested to explore the Donna, Mum and Dad dialogue (Chapter 1, pages 9–18, Lesson Idea One: Decision Making) will help you lead this discussion.

4. Students read the selected poem or extract and (in groups) answer the questions below:

a) Does the poem contain any elements of argument? (Responses could identify argument indicator words. In the case of a war poem, students are likely to say that the poem persuades them of the evils of war.)

b) Does that make the poem an argument? (Almost definitely not, since it is unlikely to contain an argument conclusion, but working this out for themselves will reinforce students' understanding of the characteristics of an argument and their ability to differentiate between argument and non-argument.)

Lesson Idea Two: comparing and contrasting two poems

General discussion

In this activity students compare and contrast two selected poems that deal with aspects of the same theme; e.g.:

- *War:* Jessie Pope 'Who's for the Game?' and Wilfred Owen 'Anthem for Doomed Youth'.
- *Dying and death:* Dylan Thomas 'Do Not Go Gentle Into That Good Night' and Christina Rossetti 'Song' or W. H. Auden 'Twelve Songs IX – Stop All The Clocks'.
- *Love:* Leonard Cohen 'Suzanne Takes You Down' and William Shakespeare Sonnet 18.
- *Human existence:* Percy Bysshe Shelley '*Prometheus Unbound – To suffer woes which Hope thinks infinite*' and Louis MacNeice '*Bagpipe Music*'.

Tasks

Students read the selected poems, then, in pairs or small groups, they consider the following questions:

a) In what ways are the two poems similar?

b) In what ways are the two poems different?

c) Explain whether these similarities and differences are significant.

d) Describe any patterns in the similarities and differences.

e) What conclusions can you draw?

Lesson Idea Three: assessing the use of analogy

General discussion

Assessing the use of analogy in a text is a problematic area for students. As students of literature they should be familiar with its use as a literary or rhetorical device and be aware that metaphors and similes are forms of analogy. They are likely to be less familiar with the use of analogy as a form of reasoning. Analogy is used to support the arguer's claim by demonstrating that two things have similarities or common characteristics, from which it is argued or inferred that a particular characteristic of one thing is also applicable to the other.

When students identify an analogy in the text, they will need to work out:

- what exactly is being compared with what (usually the bit students find difficult);

and to apply critical thinking skills:

- whether the analogy is used purely for literary effect, or whether it is also a step in a reasoning process;
- whether any particular claim is supported by the analogy and whether the analogy provides strong or weak support.

Tasks

1 a) Students are asked to identify the analogy in the gloomy 'seven ages of man' monologue in Shakespeare's *As You Like It* (Act II, Scene 7), in which men and women are compared to players (actors) upon a theatre stage, with the stages (ages) in a person's life likened to acts in a play. The analogy is sustained through to 'Last scene of all ... oblivion'.

1 b) Students discuss whether or not there is an argument within the monologue.

2. John Donne's 'A Valediction: Forbidding Mourning' could be used as the basis of a similar task.

Lesson Idea Four: credibility

Once again, Shakespeare provides us with material for critical thinking tasks. Here, students use credibility criteria to consider which is the more credible of the protagonists:

- *Julius Caesar* – Cassius, Mark Antony or Brutus?
- *The Merchant of Venice* – Antonio or Shylock?
- *Antony and Cleopatra* – Octavius or Antony?

Students may need reminding that assessing credibility does not establish which protagonist is right; it merely enables a judgement to be made as to which is more believable.

Dilemmas and ethical reasoning within English literature

Dramatic tragedies present us with conflict between the central character and the world around them, with some defect in the central character (e.g. Macbeth's ambition, Hamlet's indecisiveness, Othello's pride and jealousy, Lear's pessimism) leading to inevitable undoing. In Shakespeare's tragedies the conflict often involves the lead character having to choose between moral duty and ambition or desire for revenge. Students' critical thinking can be developed by exploring ethical reasoning frameworks and applying them to the dilemma faced by the character. This type of exercise will develop students' abilities to:

- identify the dilemma;
- understand selected ethical frameworks;
- clarify terms;

- apply one or more ethical theories to the dilemma and evaluate possible approaches;
- construct and present their own argument about the dilemma presented in the text;
- reach a reasoned judgement as to how the dilemma can best be resolved.

Ethical reasoning activities work well as class or group discussion. If this is followed up with written work, students may need to be reminded that they are *reasoning hypothetically about fictional characters*. (A sure way to irritate an examiner is to write about characters in the literary text as though they are real people. Guaranteed to irritate the examiner even more is the student who writes about the author in a matey tone: 'William shows us how Hamlet …' Students taking Advanced Level examinations in any subject should be aware that examiners expect them to follow the academic convention of referring to an author by his or her surname.)

Textual analysis

Advanced (Level 3 and above) literature syllabuses often require students to understand and apply theories of literary criticism. Producing a Marxist (or feminist or post-modern or whatever) analysis of a selected extract means students learn about Marxist (or whatever) theories of literary criticism, understand how to read literary texts, apply Marxist (or whatever) ideas to the text, and – where critical thinking skills come to the fore – construct and present their own argument about the text.

Tips to help literature students develop their critical thinking

The tips can be given to students as a handout towards the start of the course.

Tips

- The questions that occur to you while you read the text are likely to reflect the key problems and issues of the subject. Jot these questions down while you read the text. Be ready to bring your questions to class.
- If you are expected to incorporate the critical commentaries of others into your essays, then your teacher will introduce such interpretations in class. This does not necessarily mean that you need to have studied the work of academic critics in great depth, or even that you need to remember the name of the

critic. Follow your teacher's guidance on this. Make sure you can explain different interpretations. Reach you own view by synthesising different perspectives and then present your own view confidently.

- Always apply the examiner's classic adage 'Don't tell, show' by presenting reasons and evidence that lead to conclusions to produce a persuasive and cogent argument.

Religious studies

The starting point needs to be a decision as to whether the course is primarily about religious studies, in which case the critical thinking exercises will help students' analysis, evaluation, essay writing etc. However, if the development of critical thinking is the key objective, then lesson content should draw on religious studies alongside material of general interest and topics from other disciplines.

Religious studies syllabuses currently on offer cover a wide range of religious perspectives and topics. Topics likely to provide fertile ground for nurturing critical thinking skills are religious belief, religion and ethics, philosophy of religion, psychology and sociology of religion, and religion in contemporary society.

Religious studies lends itself to the development of critical thinking skills in four main ways:

- Common arguments for or against the key teachings of the faith being studied are analysed and evaluated. There are opportunities here for identifying reasons, conclusions, flaws, analogies, hypothetical reasoning, and credibility exercises.
- The teachings of the faith being studied provide a framework for ethical reasoning activities.
- The different status of belief and knowledge, and whether we can have knowledge of religious matters, are explored.
- Reasoning to support views is developed.

Critical thinking lessons should encourage students to question and discuss beliefs and ideas, but delivering critical thinking through religious studies gives rise to particular challenges. Careful classroom management may be needed: for some students winning an argument (in the non-technical sense) becomes more important than applying critical thinking skills to an issue of belief. The ground rules on page 138 should be reiterated.

Activities

The suggestions in this section are based around the Christian faith for no other reason than that the authors are more familiar with this than with other faiths.

Applying critical thinking to a passage from the sacred text

Activities based around the application of critical thinking skills to extracts from the sacred texts, or other writings on that faith, demand a highly sensitive approach on the part of the teacher. However, sacred books do contain passages of sustained reasoning Within the Christian Bible, the writings of St Paul and of James (Chapter 2) are just some opportunities for the exercise of critical thinking.

The big questions

Religious studies offers an abundance of discussion questions that allow students to practise critical thinking skills, for example:

- Is there a God?
- Is there life after death?
- What is the purpose of life?
- Why does God allow suffering?
- What is God like? (See www.philosophersnet.com/games/whatisgod.php for a 'Do-it-yourself god' activity.)

Activity: the design argument

Paley's argument for the existence of God, based on the idea of the watchmaker, is summarised below. Explain the argument to students, who should then write it out themselves as a structured argument, labelling the different elements (reasons, evidence, conclusion).

> **William Paley's argument from design**
> Many natural things in the world appear to have been designed, such as a sunflower. The human eye is very complex and could not have made itself. The watch is like the human eye. A watch is a complex mechanism, which has been made by a watchmaker. Something must have designed and made the human eye. The design seen in nature and the universe is not an accident (e.g. of evolution). Therefore, a thinking creator being (God) exists.

Comment

Another approach would be to split the argument into sentences, which are given to students on separate cards. Alternatively, you could muddle up the order of the sentences and present them on a whiteboard. Students rearrange them into a structured order and decide which component of the argument each sentence represents. Students' responses need not necessarily be in the same order as the structure above, but they should still have identified the elements correctly.

This activity could also be used to introduce (or remind students of) some critical thinking concepts:

- additional evidence: students suggest other examples of natural things that appear to have been designed;
- reasons acting jointly or separately;
- analogy: students consider the strength, or otherwise, of the use of the analogy of the watch;
- students write their own arguments to counter Paley's design argument.

Students could move on to analyse the structure of other arguments for, or against, the existence of God. The main arguments for God's existence (ontological: argument from being; teleological: argument from design; cosmological; moral; religious experience) offer opportunities for students to practise critical thinking through different activities:

- In pairs, students write out one of the arguments for God's existence as a short, reasoned argument.
- The pairs swap their argument with another pair. Each pair writes out a short argument that counters the one they have received.
- Students work in pairs to identify strengths and weaknesses of a selected argument. This could form the basis of a home-work task in which students present their own judgement on the strengths and weaknesses of the chosen argument for or against the existence of God.

Lesson Idea Five: credibility: the Gospel sources

Teaching about Gospel sources can take on a new dimension when critical thinking is integrated. Topics which could be explored within a credibility framework include:

- the Gospel writers' purposes and intended readership;
- questions of authorship and sources;
- historical documents or theology.

Lesson Idea Six: credibility – the resurrection of Jesus

The Gospel accounts of the resurrection of Jesus can be tackled as a straight credibility exercise or as a whodunnit. Select from Matthew 28, Mark 16, Luke 23:50–24:12 (for eyewitness evidence), Luke 24 and John 20.

Students can apply the credibility criteria to the sources and participants (the Gospel writers, the women, Peter, the other disciples, guards, Roman authorities). For the classic exposition of the narratives, albeit from a personal perspective, try Frank Morrison's *Who Moved the Stone* (in print since 1930 and obtainable new or second-hand; publisher Faber and Faber).

A whodunnit approach will provide opportunities for the exercise of hypothetical reasoning, for example:

- If Joseph of Arimathea had removed the body, then he would swiftly have let Jesus' followers know what he had done.
- If the Romans had taken the body away and buried it, then they would soon have stopped any rumours by announcing what they had done with the body;

and so on with the other explanations:

- the disciples stole the body to make it look as though Jesus had risen from the dead;
- Jesus wasn't really dead – he went into a coma and then woke up;
- the women could not see clearly because of grief or because it was early morning;
- the women went to the wrong tomb.

Ethical reasoning activities

Activity One: genetic screening

Background information for students:

Most religious teaching emphasises the sanctity of life and that life starts at conception. It also teaches that the sick and disabled are equally valuable to God. Christians, for example, refer to Psalm 39 to justify this belief.

Couples who know there is a risk of them having a child with certain inherited conditions may now be able to have embryos tested for those diseases. A number of embryos are created in the laboratory through *in vitro* fertilisation (IVF). The clinic can test the embryos to see if they carry a specific genetic mutation such as cystic fibrosis. An embryo that does not carry the mutation is selected for implantation in the mother's womb. Those that do carry it can be destroyed or frozen. Karyomapping, a new test, might mean embryos can be screened for possible future heart disease or cancer.

Questions for discussion

- Is a child a right or a gift?
- When does the embryo become a person?
- Does the right to life of the foetus have greater importance than the right of the mother to choose what happens with her body?
- Does this type of screening deny respect and equality to people with learning or physical disabilities?
- If you decide to screen for some conditions, but not others, how do you decide which embryos to select?

Activity Two: symbols of religion

Governments, schools and companies have made different decisions about whether or not people should be allowed to wear symbols of religion at their place of study or work. Students could carry out their own research on how different countries have dealt with this, using this as a basis for group discussion. Symbols of religion often worn are headscarves, Christian symbols such as crosses and fish jewellery, and Sikh bracelets. What should be accepted? Where do you draw the line – should Sikhs be allowed to carry ritual swords?

Activity Three: cheque-book journalism and individuals' right to privacy

You could make this topic relevant by providing students with one or two recent newspaper stories about popular celebrities misbehaving (e.g. a footballer who has been unfaithful to his wife, or a celebrity caught using drugs, etc.). If the celebrity has complained about press intrusion, so much the better. As a contrast, students could be given an account of someone working in a public sector job who has made false expense claims. (*Private Eye*'s 'Rotten Boroughs' column contains plenty of these stories.) You could also use the information about the UK MPs' expenses scandal given below.

Start this activity by trying to get students to work out what 'in the public interest' means. They might suggest freedom of expression is in the public interest, or that something is in the public interest when the possible damage to a number of people is greater than the harm to the one person whom the story would hurt.

Background information for students

The *Daily Telegraph* is believed to have paid a large sum of money for the information it revealed in May 2009 about expenses claimed by UK MPs. Although there were already plans to make public the amount of MPs' expense claims, this would not have revealed as much detail as the *Telegraph* printed. The *Telegraph* claimed the story was a triumph for old-style journalism, which involved days of research by a team of journalists. Circulation of the *Telegraph* increased while this story was running.

Questions for discussion

Were the examples students studied just cheque-book journalism or genuinely in the public interest?

Do famous people have a right to privacy? How far does that right go? How far is media intrusion into people's private lives justified by the public interest? Should the media reveal some forms of wrongdoing but not others? If so, which?

Activity Four: presenting an ethical reasoning case

There is a wealth of topics that students could research independently as preparation for presenting their own case on an issue within an ethical framework. A few suggestions are given below.

- *Euthanasia:* In the UK, self-suicide is acceptable, but helping someone to commit suicide is illegal. Should the law be changed?
- *Abortion:* If intervention to sustain the embryo's life is accepted, why is intervention to end it not accepted?
- *Industrial action:* Should health workers, police officers and fire officers be allowed the right to strike?
- *International pharmaceutical companies:* How can the need to make a profit to fund expensive research into new drugs be reconciled with the need of poorer countries for drugs, such as treatment for HIV (AIDS).
- *Retirement age:* Should everyone be forced to retire at 65?

- If God created the universe, is God then liable for whatever happens in it?
- Is morality dependent on (belief in) God?
- Some ape species and people share 98.4 per cent of the same genetic make-up. If we have a soul, do apes and chimpanzees also have one?
- How far does belief in miracles imply that God is arbitrary and partisan?
- To what extent is conscience a sound basis for ethical decision making?

Science and mathematics subjects

So far this chapter has looked at integrating thinking skills within subjects where the important (and interesting) questions do not have definitive answers. In science and mathematics, there is greater expectation that answers are certain and unambiguous (although this is less the case at the forefront of research). Many science and mathematics teachers take the view that studying these subjects implicitly develops students' critical thinking. This is somewhat simplistic: practising mathematical manipulation requires logical thought and certainly improves students' ability to perform mathematical manipulations. It is less effective than practising critical thinking skills in improving their reasoning skills.

That said, mathematics and science students tend to perform well in thinking skills assessments that test problem solving. Furthermore, there is evidence of a high correlation between success in examinations in science subjects and success in critical thinking assessments – when the students have had relevant examination preparation. There appear to be similarities between the cognitive processes required in a critical thinking task and those developed through the study of science and mathematics subjects. Critical thinking's methods replicate science's investigative methods: the question is articulated, the hypothesis is formulated and tested, evidence is interpreted, and conclusions are drawn. If the critical thinking is about drawing sound conclusions based on reasoning and evidence, then it has much in common with science. The positive dispositions that critical thinking develops (outlined in Chapter 6 on page 127) include openness to new ideas, intellectual independence, willingness to challenge accepted ideas in the light of evidence and argument, and ability to recognise connections and base conclusions on sound evidence and reasons. These are also the dispositions required for scientific research.

As discussed above, successfully integrating thinking and reasoning skills within a subject involves a questioning and problem-solving approach. Scientific enquiry is about investigating problems: science teachers already possess the necessary skills, which can be applied to teach critical thinking.

Tips for integrating thinking skills in science courses

1. If students are to be entered for a critical thinking examination, then they need to become familiar with reasoning presented through language as well as in customary scientific formats. They also need to learn the terminology and methods of critical thinking. There is no reason why this cannot be done using science-based material. The BMAT specimen paper can be obtained and will provide some ideas (see www.admissionstests.cambridgeassessment.org.uk/adt/).

2. Until relatively recently, science was intellectually closer to philosophy than it is now considered to be. Encourage students to enter into discussion by relating lesson topics to their historical and philosophical links. This will also introduce students to the realisation that knowledge and facts are not fixed and that new research leads to the re-evaluation of previous work.

3. Use questioning techniques in class that stimulate critical thinking, for example:

   - What data are needed to answer this question?
   - How can the data be used to answer the question?
   - What might explain this result?
   - What can be inferred from this?

4. Thinking skills assessments deal with material presented mainly through text, but also as data. Writing tasks, which need not be lengthy essays, will develop students' critical thinking, because they have to get to grips with the topic, organise their material, and present their ideas persuasively. For example, allocate ten minutes at the end of lessons for students to write a short summary, say around 70 words, of the most important thing they have learnt in that class.

5. Avoid setting homework questions that focus on recall of factual knowledge. Students need to engage with the information rather than just regurgitate it. Occasional homework tasks could ask them to summarise a scientific article (e.g. from *New Scientist* or Ben Goldacre's Bad Science column in the *Guardian* (downloadable from www.guardian.co.uk/science/series/badscience). Alternatively,

they could review the type of popular science article that sullies even the BBC's website (see http://news.bbc.co.uk/1/hi/sci/tech/default.stm) and the pages of broadsheet newspapers.

Vocational subjects (business, sports studies, etc.)

Many vocational courses provide rich opportunities for integrating thinking skills by tweaking the content and demand of typical case study or in-tray tasks to provide opportunities for:

- evaluating data;
- evaluating a business case including assessing and interpreting evidence, identifying flaws and weaknesses;
- ethical business decision making;
- report writing – making a reasoned business case;
- preparing and delivering a presentation – constructing a reasoned argument containing evidence, reasons and conclusion.

Business-related tasks that develop thinking skills stimulate debate and require judgements to be made, but do not have obvious right or wrong answers.

Lesson idea

Suitably contextualised, this activity could be adapted for courses in a variety of vocational subjects: leisure and tourism, business, performing arts or retail. It should ideally be based on a real proposal for a development that is relevant to the vocational area and has provoked some local opposition. Relevant development proposals could be: demolition of an old/attractive building and its replacement with a sports centre, car park or shopping centre; housing development (either social housing or using greenfield land for private development of large houses); relocation of a bus shelter; pedestrianisation of a local road of shops making parking difficult; open-cast mining; or building factories on farmland.

Part (b) should be introduced using class discussion to identify groups or individuals whose interests are being served in this situation, and how they are being advantaged. Students also need to identify those who are being disadvantaged in the situation. (These could be people living nearby who will be affected by traffic and noise, people seeking work, environmentalists, walkers, and people who enjoy open spaces.) This could lead into wider discussion about the importance and cultural significance of the vocational area (e.g. sport, leisure, tourism, retail) for individuals and social groups. Students could also examine the values, cultures, attitudes and beliefs that underpin attitudes towards and participation in sport, leisure activities, etc.

Instructions for students

a) Use local newspapers and websites to research the proposed development and the expected benefits and disadvantages.

b) Identify at least three different groups of people who will be affected positively or adversely by the proposed development. Explain how each group will be affected and their different perspectives on the development.

c) Recommend whether the proposed development should go ahead, not go ahead or go ahead with certain conditions. Support your recommendation with reasons and evidence.

Tools for Assessment

Introduction to Part 3

Developing the skill of thinking critically, and applying that skill in life, work and study, is a worthwhile end in itself, but tests and examinations are an unavoidable necessity in most education systems. The purpose of assessment is to provide information on progress made by students during a programme of study, and on the knowledge, skills and abilities acquired. Thinking skills assessments make unique demands on candidates because they test cognitive skills rather than knowledge of subject content. Preparing students presents teachers with unusual challenges. Part 3 will help you select the right thinking skills assessment or qualification for your students, prepare them for the examination, deal with examination boards' requirements, and decide what action to take if results are disappointing.

8 Preparing for Assessment

This chapter includes:

- an overview of the main public examinations in thinking skills available at the time of writing in the UK, USA, Australia and elsewhere;
- guidance on selecting the assessment that will best meet your students' needs;
- guidance on managing external examinations;
- an outline of different question types used to assess thinking skills;
- advice on the common areas where students go wrong;
- tips for students.

High-stakes Thinking Skills Examinations

There are broadly three types of potentially high-stakes thinking skills examinations that students may attempt:

- Assessments that lead to a *qualification* (certificate) at the end of a course of study. Qualifications that certificate thinking skills or critical thinking as a 'standalone' subject are gaining in popularity in the UK, and in some countries whose education systems have been influenced by the UK. Also available are qualifications that certificate critical thinking alongside other subjects or generic skills.[10]
- *Tests* that assess thinking skills as part of a selection process for university courses or, less commonly, for employment; use of these tests is widespread in the USA, Australia and a small number of elite UK universities.
- *Tests* of thinking skills taken at different stages during a course of study of a different subject for *diagnostic* purposes or to assess performance over time; these are quite popular with some US and Australian universities.

The assessments considered in this chapter are publicly available tests or examinations, set and marked by a body external to the school or college that prepares the students for the assessment.

Thinking skills qualifications and assessments

Most assessments in discrete thinking skills are designed for students in the pre-university phase of education and take the form of external tests or examinations, rather than tutor-marked coursework assignments. (The exceptions are noted below.) In the USA, where there is longer experience of assessing thinking skills and critical thinking than elsewhere, many universities have made tests such as the Scholastic Aptitude Tests (SATs) a mandatory requirement for applicants, because they can provide a benchmark indicator of a student's academic ability. This is in part a recognition that the standard of high school leaving certificates and diplomas is inconsistent across states, because each state manages its own system. In an attempt to address this inconsistency (some would say unreliability), work has begun on national standards for US high school diplomas, but in the meantime the outcomes of critical thinking assessments continue to be treated as providing significant, relevant information on the university applicant.

Australia has followed a similar route to the USA: the Australian Council for Education Research (ACER) offers a range of generic skills (including thinking skills) assessments for general university selection, for selection to specific courses and for monitoring students' generic skills performance during or at the end of an academic course. ACER now markets its products in a number of other countries, including India.

The pattern in most European countries is that students' results detailed in their respective school-leaving certificate are sufficient to gain a university place. UK universities select applicants on the basis of projected or actual results in General Certificate of Education (GCE) Advanced Level subjects (or National Qualifications in Scotland, which has a different system). The UK qualifications system is highly regulated by government agencies and there is a relatively high level of confidence in the consistency of the standards of qualifications. The UK is unusual in that critical thinking can be taken as a qualification in its own right, equal in weight and status to other academic subjects. A small number of UK universities require applicants to sit tests of general aptitude or thinking skills; these tend to be elite institutions and faculties, which can select from large numbers of high-calibre applicants. Many UK universities regard possession of a GCE Critical Thinking qualification as an indicator of academic potential.

Issues in the assessment of thinking skills

On the face of it, assessing students' thinking skills ought to be comparable with assessing any skills-based subject. A tutor assessing a student's skill at painting (whether pictures or walls) can watch the *process* – how the student handles paint and brushes – and see the final *outcome* or *product*. Marks or grades can be assigned for both process and outcome. The thinking skills examiner can assess a product, whether it is a solution to a problem, a critical analysis of reasoning, the student's own reasoned argument, or evidence that the student has carried out some process of reflective thinking. What the examiner cannot assess is the thinking processes that resulted in the product, except in so far as this becomes visible through the product.

Assessment of problem solving through tasks based around manipulation of data and information is fairly well tried and tested. Thinking skills and critical thinking, on the other hand, are subjects where experience in assessment has developed relatively recently – in the case of the UK, since 1999 – and examination boards are still developing expertise. Until recently, there was a cautious view in the UK that the newness of critical thinking as a taught subject meant that teachers did not yet have sufficient expertise to create and mark critical thinking coursework assessments reliably enough for high-stakes assessments (i.e. advanced or Level 3 and leading to university entrance). CIE's International GCSE in Global Perspectives (Level 2), however, contains a teacher-marked coursework component – a development with wider potential.

Most current critical thinking examinations are based predominantly around material of general interest presented through text. Such material is inevitably open to differing interpretations. It has taken time to understand the problems arising from the tension between the imprecision of everyday communication and the impact on examining of the extreme precision demanded by philosophical methods. There has been a variety of attempted solutions to these problems: tasks and mark schemes that take a rather rigid, mechanistic approach alongside trials of different ways of marking critical thinking, whereby alternative interpretations of textual material can be credited. At the same time, examiners are attempting to avoid the subjective element of, say, humanities essay marking. (If you think you could do this, examination boards are ready and waiting for your application to be an examiner.)

The inherent difficulties in reducing subjectivity in marking are not unique to thinking skills: examination boards have long recognised that it is easier to achieve consistency of marking in mathematics or accounting than in literature or history.

A particular feature of thinking skills assessments is that, unlike in most other subjects, candidates do not bring a body of subject knowledge into the examination room with them. The material they have to think about has to be provided, either as pre-release material, or as material to plough through before they get to the questions. A less common alternative is that candidates pre-select their own material. The types of assessment task and questions that can be set may be limited by the way the material is provided.

Question types

The issues that arise in assessment of thinking skills impact on task and question types. Those that students are more likely to encounter are considered below.

Multiple choice items

Many students prefer multiple choice tests, especially if their skills in written language do not match their thinking skills. The disadvantage is that candidates usually have to read a fair amount of complex material (which may be text and data) before they can answer the questions. Multiple choice tests are highly cost-effective where there are high candidate numbers because they can be created from a large bank of items and machine marking is cheaper than human examiners, so this option is often used in tests run on a commercial basis. Data on every question in the item bank, derived from previous or trial test sessions, can be used to build tests with a very high level of consistency and reliability.

Multiple choice questions are used extensively in tests employed to select university applicants, usually to assess problem solving and critical thinking. They are also used for discrete testing of specific critical thinking skills, such as identifying reasons, assumptions, conclusions that can be drawn, flaws and weaknesses.

Multiple choice questions have drawbacks. First, they do not discriminate between the candidate who gives serious thought as to which is the right answer and the candidate who just guesses or has been successfully trained to spot the formula. They cannot be used to assess some higher-level thinking, such as producing one's own reasoning. Nor do they allow for differing interpretations whereby a candidate chooses the 'wrong' answer, based on 'good', even sophisticated, thinking, which happens not to be the same as the question-writer's thinking.

Short-answer questions

Short-answer questions are often presented in a structured way, so that candidates start with more straightforward questions and build up to questions requiring more complex responses. Again, students usually have to work their way through some material before they get to the questions, which can test a wide range of skills, including identifying reasons, assumptions, conclusions and flaws; analysis of argument; assessing evidence, analogy, credibility; and assessing the strength or weakness of an argument. Some of the most challenging questions require students to develop their own reasoning making critical use of source material provided (i.e. building on their analysis and evaluation answers).

Questions requiring extended answers

These provide opportunities for candidates to demonstrate the full range of skills, including producing their own original arguments, providing a full analysis or evaluation of an argument, or exploring different perspectives on an issue or problem.

Examined coursework and teacher-marked coursework

CIE offers several thinking skills syllabuses, including Global Perspectives and Independent Research Report, IGCSE Global Perspectives, and Knowledge and Inquiry, which are assessed through more than one method, including coursework. Students work independently to produce an essay, presentation, portfolio, project report or independent research study. These are marked according to the level of thinking and reasoning skills demonstrated by students in terms of understanding and representing issues from different perspectives, analysis, evaluation and development of reasoning. The coursework is either examiner-marked or teacher-marked, as is more appropriate for the level.

Guide to the leading thinking skills assessments

In this section, leading thinking skills and critical thinking assessments are reviewed. The qualifications and assessments considered are those examined through the medium of English that attract significant numbers of student entries. Some assessments have been included that, at the time of writing, attract relatively fewer entries, but look likely to become more popular or represent a significant or innovative development in thinking skills assessment. They have been grouped according to the three types of assessment outlined in the introduction to this chapter on page 163. In addition, Ennis' three different categories of critical thinking test, based on two criteria (Ennis, 1996), have been found to provide a useful framework. Ennis' categories were based on:

- whether content was general or subject specific; and,
- whether a single or multiple critical thinking aspects (or skills) were assessed.

This overview is not exhaustive: much like any consumer product, tests and qualifications can be withdrawn or redesigned. Before students are prepared for a particular examination, it is essential that you read the up-to-date syllabus together with sample papers, mark schemes and examiners' reports on previous examinations. You also need to check current regulations and scheduled exam dates.

Assessments that lead to a qualification (certificate) in thinking skills or critical thinking at the end of a course in the subject

Qualifications at GCE (General Certificate of Education) Advanced Level

Both traditional academic and vocational qualifications can meet the minimum requirements for entrance to UK universities, but the 'gold standard' in the UK, and in some countries with historic links with the UK, remains the General Certificate of Education at Advanced Level (GCE A Level) qualification. This is usually taken at the end of year 13. The first half of the GCE A Level course can lead to a lower-level qualification, the General Certificate of Education at Advanced Subsidiary (GCE AS), usually achieved at the end of year 12. (NB: Scotland has a different school qualifications system to the rest of the UK.)

CIE GCE (International Syllabus) Advanced Level and Advanced Subsidiary Level Thinking Skills

CIE (Cambridge International Examinations) offers this qualification outside the UK and candidates are entered from countries worldwide, many of which have worked with CIE for decades, but developed their own distinctive curriculum. CIE is part of Cambridge Assessment, the UK's leading source of expertise in thinking skills assessment and a department of Cambridge University; accordingly, CIE qualifications are respected globally. Teachers delivering CIE qualifications have access to training and support in the form of previous examination papers, mark schemes, examiner reports, online teacher forums, 'ask the examiner' sessions, and both face-to-face and online training.

Both problem solving (data handling, modelling and analysis) and critical thinking are assessed, and the questions papers are based around material of general interest. The examinations are taken in a linear style at the end of the AS or A Level course respectively. Candidates for the full A Level take four papers, which each contribute 25 per cent of the final grade. Pass results are graded on a scale of A–E.

To achieve CIE GCE AS Thinking Skills candidates take:

Paper 1: Problem Solving containing 30 multiple choice questions based on short passages of stimulus material.

Paper 2: Critical Reasoning requiring the candidate to evaluate evidence, to engage in reasoning in a scientific context, to evaluate an argument in a passage of about 350 words and to present an argument.

Additionally, to achieve the full GCE Advanced Level, candidates take two further papers:

Paper 3: Problem Solving containing questions based on information in text, graphical and/or numerical form, requiring longer answers.

Paper 4: Applied Reasoning containing short-answer and essay questions, requiring candidates to develop a model or carry out an investigation, analyse information and draw conclusions, and to select from given information, opinion and/or argument in several documents and use this to construct a reasoned case.

OCR Advanced Level and Advanced Subsidiary Level Critical Thinking (UK)

In 1998, OCR (Oxford Cambridge and RSA) developed an Advanced Subsidiary in Critical Thinking in a joint project with the National Foundation for Educational Research (NFER). GCE AS Critical Thinking was designed specifically for UK schools and colleges, but was built on expertise in the assessment of thinking skills provided by OCR's sister organisation CIE. OCR's Advanced Subsidiary has grown from a few hundred candidate entries in 1998 to around 25,000 in 2009. Since 2006, UK students have had the opportunity to achieve a full GCE A Level in Critical Thinking.

Many candidates for OCR's Critical Thinking regard it as their fourth- or even fifth-choice subject, which provides curriculum breadth and enrichment in year 12. The vast majority do not carry on to take the full A Level. It is not entirely clear whether students opt out, or whether schools do not yet feel equipped to offer critical thinking to the full A Level standard.

One attraction of offering the OCR qualification is that OCR is part of Cambridge Assessment, so is supported by considerable expertise in the assessment of thinking skills. In addition, plenty of support is available for this qualification in the form of textbooks, resource materials, training events, past question papers, mark schemes and examiner reports.

Some teachers have suggested that the OCR syllabus takes an excessively formulaic approach to assessment of the skills, particularly in Units 1 and 2. On the other hand, this makes the subject accessible to students who might struggle with more open-ended tasks. This qualification is unitised (modular), so the examinations for the four units can be taken in stages or, if preferred, at the end of the course of study. Modular courses provide flexibility and students are reassured by knowing that they can retake units where they have performed less well, and their best result will count towards the final grade. However, if they are studying several subjects on a modular basis, they can be overloaded by examinations. Pass results are graded on a scale of A*–E.

Candidates for OCR GCE AS Critical Thinking take:

Unit 1: Introduction to Critical Thinking, covering the language of reasoning and credibility.

Unit 2: Assessing and Developing Argument, assessing analysis and evaluation of argument, and developing one's own reasoned arguments.

Additionally, to achieve the full OCR GCE A Level Critical Thinking, candidates take:

Unit 3: Ethical Reasoning and Decision-making, which involves ethical theories, recognising and applying principles, and dilemmas and decision making.

Unit 4: Critical Reasoning, which covers analysis, evaluation and development of complex arguments.

The Assessment and Qualification Alliance's (AQA) A Level Critical Thinking was offered for the first time in 2009. At first sight, it is a challenging qualification, but it could be attractive to teachers looking for an alternative to OCR's approach. The syllabus content is wide ranging and demanding: probability and statistical reasoning in Unit 2 may worry some teachers and students. Like OCR GCE Critical Thinking, the AQA qualification is unitised (modular) and Pass results are graded on a scale of A*–E.

Candidates for AQA GCE AS Critical Thinking take:

Unit 1: Critical Thinking Foundation Unit introduces elements of argument, including analogies, assumptions, flaws and fallacies.

Unit 2: Information, Inference and Explanation includes assessment of evidence, credibility, statistical reasoning, explanations and inference. Candidates argue for or against a proposal on a topic related to source material.

Additionally to achieve AQA GCE A Level Critical Thinking, candidates take:

Unit 3: Beliefs, Claims and Arguments covering knowledge and belief, kinds of evidence used to justify beliefs and claims, probability, strong and weak claims, hypothesis testing, prediction, patterns of reasoning, suppositional reasoning, argument from analogy, basic logical ideas, ethical arguments and principles.

Unit 4: Reasoning and Decision Making, covers decision-making strategies, including data handling, probability theory and decision trees. The examination is based on pre-release material and additional material provided in the examination.

SQA (Scottish Qualifications Authority) National Units

Schools and colleges in Scotland have access to SQA National Qualifications. Optional Critical Thinking units at Intermediate and Advanced can be delivered as part of Philosophy courses. The SQA provides some limited guidance material. Teachers delivering these units could consider using textbooks and resources designed for GCE A Level Critical Thinking.

Singapore Ministry of Education Knowledge and Inquiry
This is available only to Singapore institutions, with the expertise in thinking skills assessment provided by CIE.

CIE Level 3 Pre-U Diploma and CIE Pre-U Certificate in Global Perspectives and Independent Research
Cambridge Assessment's Pre-U Diploma was initially offered within the UK only. At the time of writing, CIE had invited non-UK schools to express their interest in offering the qualification. If you are considering teaching this in a non-UK institution, it is essential that you check the up-to-date position with CIE (website: www.cie.org.uk).

The Pre-U Diploma package offers a framework for a broadly based, academically rigorous course of study in preparation for university. Alternatively, schools can prepare their students for individual components of the qualification instead of the complete Diploma. A course in thinking and reasoning skills could be built around the two compulsory core components of the Pre-U Diploma, which would enable students to achieve the CIE Level 3 Pre-U Certificate in Global Perspectives and Independent Research. Alternatively, Global Perspectives can be taken and certificated as a standalone unit. The recommended guided learning hours are 200 for Global Perspectives and 120 for Independent Research.

The Global Perspectives part of the course aims to develop students' thinking, reasoning and research skills through five key themes based around issues of global relevance: ethics, economics, environment, technology, and politics and culture. As well as analysis and evaluation within a global context, Global Perspectives also claims to assess candidates' dispositions.

Global Perspectives is assessed through three examiner-marked components: a written examination based around analysis of perspectives contained in two passages (25 per cent), a 1,500-word essay (30 per cent), and – unusually – a multi-media presentation (45 per cent). Pass results are graded on a scale of nine grades: Distinction 1 (above Advanced Level A* grade), 2 and 3 (aligned to Grade A at Advanced Level), Merit 1, 2 and 3, and Pass 1, 2 and 3 (aligned to Grade E at Advanced Level).

Independent Research builds on the skills developed through Global Perspectives and is assessed through a 4,500-word report on a topic chosen by the candidate in consultation with their teacher.

Cambridge Skills Development Programme (SDP)
CIE collaborated with the European Union Education Foundation (CHEER) to develop and validate a programme that will enable

students from mainland China to engage in academic study in Western universities and business. The programme is designed to help students develop presentation and communication skills, ability to think and reason in contexts, independent, reflective learning, teamwork, and their ability to engage in enterprise. Thinking skills are one of several strands, and they are embedded in context, combined with some explicit teaching, in order that students learn to apply them in a meaningful way. The course normally involves 120 hours of full-time study at approved schools in China, and successful completion leads to the Cambridge SDP Certificate.

Assessment is not through traditional examination, but through a combination of peer assessment, a reflective log, project management and a final individual presentation.

OCR Level 2 Award in Thinking and Reasoning Skills (UK)

This award is offered within the UK and is designed to be taught in around 60 hours. It is aimed primarily at students aged 14–16, although it could also be used with older students, and as preparation for higher-level thinking skills courses. The skills are developed through topics such as crime and antisocial behaviour, drugs and alcohol abuse, ethical issues, animal welfare, freedom of expression and tolerance, civil disobedience, global warming, poverty, life after death, astrology, and alleged supernatural experiences. The skills assessed are: analysis, evaluation, synthesis, problem solving, information processing, and creative thinking. Assessment is through two examinations. In the first, candidates tackle short-answer questions and longer structured questions based around one or two sources. The second examination is based on pre-released material and contains short-answer questions and a response to an argument.

Tests that assess thinking skills as part of a selection process for university courses or for employment

In the USA, it is customary for university applicants to take commercially designed tests that assess critical thinking through the medium of English and mathematics, and Australia follows this pattern. 'Russell Group' members including Oxford and Cambridge increasingly require applicants to take thinking skills or critical thinking tests to enable differentiation between a large number of high-calibre applicants.

Australian Council of Education Research (ACER) UniTest

ACER provides a very wide range of tests for university entrance. Some are run for specific universities; others, such as UniTest, are offered more widely. UniTest tests problem solving and other abilities through multiple choice questions.

Cambridge University Thinking Skills Assessment (TSA)

Certain Oxford and Cambridge colleges require applicants to have taken the Thinking Skills Assessment in addition to GCE A Level examinations, and courses such as medicine, veterinary science and law have specific entrance tests that assess critical thinking or problem solving.

Law School Admission Test (LSAT) (USA)

LSAT is a standardised test developed and administered by the Law School Admissions Services (see www.lsac.org) whose admission services are used by universities in the United States, Canada, and Australia. LSAT is designed to assess applicants' potential to succeed in their first year of law school. The test comprises five sections containing multiple choice questions that assess reading comprehension, analytical reasoning and logical reasoning. Only four of the five sections contribute to the final score, with the remaining section being experimental. Candidates do not know which section is not marked. In addition there is a 30-minute writing task, which LSAC does not mark, but sends to applicants' chosen institutions. All questions are equally weighted. The LSAT score is based on the number of correct answers, without deductions for wrong answers, converted to a scale from 120 to 180.

National Admissions Test for Law (LNAT) (UK)

The LNAT is run by LNAT Consortium Ltd, which was formed by eight UK universities that offer law degrees (see www.lnat.ac.uk). The LNAT lasts two hours and is taken on-screen. The first section (80 minutes) contains 10 argumentative passages, with 3 multiple-choice questions on each, making 30 questions in total. The multiple choice part is a general-content, multi-aspect, critical thinking test. The questions are designed to test verbal reasoning skills relevant to study of law (comprehension, interpretation, analysis, synthesis, induction, and deduction), without requiring specialist knowledge other than English. This section is machine-marked. The second section (40 minutes) requires candidates to write an essay in English (500–600 words) on a topic from a list. It requires ability 'to argue economically to a conclusion with a good command of written English'.

The Bio-Medical Admissions Test (BMAT) (UK)

BMAT is a subject-specific, multi-aspect critical thinking test. It comprises a 'test of aptitude and skills', a 'test of scientific knowledge and applications'; and a short writing task. BMAT is intended to be accessible to all potential applicants irrespective of background, in that questions are designed so that no specific preparation beyond GCSE-level science and mathematics is necessary. Cambridge Assessment runs this test on behalf of seven medical and veterinary schools in England.

Graduate Medical School Admissions Test (UK)

GMAT is delivered by ACER for five UK universities to select graduates from any field for medical training. The three sections are:

Section I: Reasoning in Humanities and Social Sciences using different texts as stimulus material and visual and tabular material to assess complex verbal processing and conceptual thinking, logical and plausible reasoning, and objective and subjective thinking. Questions that emphasise critical thinking require candidates to make discriminations and judgements in the realm of plausible reasoning. Questions in this section are in multiple choice format.

Section II: Written Communication comprises two writing tasks, which assess communication and quality of thinking about a topic.

Section III: Reasoning in Biological and Physical Sciences, in addition to testing problem solving within a scientific context, examines understanding of basic science concepts. Multiple choice questions are based on stimulus material presented in verbal, mathematical, graphical and visual formats, with a focus primarily on problem solving.

Scholastic Aptitude Test (SAT) (USA)

In the USA the SAT Reasoning Test (Scholastic Aptitude Test – not be to confused with the UK's SATs) is run by Educational Testing Services (ETS) on behalf of the College Board. The College Board is an association of 5,400-plus educational organizations. Not all US higher education colleges require SATs scores, or require them only from students applying from outside the state. The SATs scores provide independent, standardised assessment of a student's critical reading, mathematical reasoning, and writing skills. SAT scores are intended to supplement the secondary school record and help admissions officers put course work, grades and class rank in a national perspective, given the variation in grading standards and course rigour within and across high schools.

Tests of thinking skills taken at different stages during a course of study of a different subject for diagnostic purposes or to assess performance over time

General content, multiple aspect tests assess a range of critical thinking skills using material of general interest. They are popular in some US universities, which use them for diagnostic purposes and to assess the 'added value' provided by the education process. They are often commercially produced and so multiple choice items are common. Several tests are available, those listed below being regarded as among the more reliable.[11]

- *The California Critical Thinking Dispositions Inventory* (1992) was developed by Peter Facione and N. C. Facione.
- *The Ennis-Weir Critical Thinking Essay Test* (1985) was developed by Robert H. Ennis and Eric Weir.
- *The Watson-Glaser Critical Thinking Appraisal* (1980) for selection for employment is available in one version of the test only and offered through Harcourt Assessment, Inc.

In addition, there are general content, aspect-specific critical thinking tests. The most significant are the *Cornell Class Reasoning Test* (1964), developed by Ennis and others for a research project, and the similar *Cornell Conditional Reasoning Test*, which also uses multiple choice items to test general critical thinking skills. See http://faculty.ed.uiuc.edu/rhennis/infocornelldedtests.htm to download the early Cornell Deduction tests, which can be used in classrooms.

Test on Appraising Observations (1983), by Stephen P. Norris and Ruth King, Department of Educational Policy Studies, University of Alberta, uses 50 test items to assess the ability of senior high school students to correctly appraise observations. See www.eric.ed.gov/ERICDocs/data/ericdocs2sql/content_storage_01/0000019b/80/32/22/ea.pdf.

Subject-specific, skill-specific tests were not identified by Ennis, but could be useful. A law case study which assessed credibility could conceivably be useful, as would a science-based test that assessed ability to identify flaws in reasoning.

Deciding which syllabus to teach

How to read the syllabus

Well before teaching starts, get hold of as much information as possible about the qualifications available. An examination board sets out its offering in its syllabuses, but these are sometimes impenetrable documents. As well as the syllabus, essential documents are a specimen paper and, ideally, past question papers, mark schemes and examiner reports from recent examinations. Together, they will enable you to work out what you actually need to teach and to get a sense of whether or not you will enjoy it. If it does not trigger your interest, then your students are unlikely to be excited by the course.

Other than when a qualification has been recently introduced, question papers from previous sessions should be obtainable, either as downloads from the board's website or in hard copy. If they are not easily obtained, then it may be a warning sign that the board is not committed to resourcing the qualification and to providing the necessary support to teachers.

The acquisition of skills to support study in other subjects, intellectual challenge, and the chance to study something different from other subjects are all worthwhile objectives, but students are essentially pragmatic: they may sign up for critical thinking simply expecting a 'quick win' extra qualification to add to their other subjects. You should treat with a pinch of salt the myths that circulate about one syllabus being 'easier' than others. Instead, get hold of the evidence: most boards publish statistical breakdowns of results in terms of Pass/Fail outcomes and percentages achieving different grades, which can be used to make comparisons. However, you should not assume that higher percentage Pass rates mean a particular syllabus is more accessible (for which read 'easier'). Pass rates reflect the ability and achievement of the whole cohort, and certain types of institution have historically been loyal to particular examination boards. UK examination boards, in particular, are highly regulated and standards across them are, in the main, remarkably consistent.

Syllabuses and past papers (plus mark schemes) should provide plenty of information to help you select the one that will best meet your students' needs, and also to prepare to teach it. Key factors to consider are outlined below.

- *Subject content:* Not only do you need to assess your own ability (or lack of it) to teach the qualification, but you also need to be realistic about your students' chances of success. If you are new to teaching this subject you may be more comfortable delivering a syllabus that focuses on a fairly narrow range of critical thinking skills assessed through structured tasks. Whilst this can be mechanistic, it can work with students who are not suited to an academic approach. The alternative may be a syllabus that demands a wider range of reasoning skills, such as decision-making techniques, probability and scientific hypothesis building. This can be daunting for teachers who are not confident about their own numeracy skills, let alone those of their students.

- *Teaching resources and support:* The teacher's life is undoubtedly easier if good support is available in the form of training, textbooks and guidance material. Availability of teaching resources is often the deciding factor when a syllabus is chosen, but you still need to be discriminating in selecting resources.
- *Form of assessment:* Some students perform better if assessment is through coursework tasks rather than examination. On the other hand, coursework may be a tedious burden for students to do and for the teacher to mark.
- *Assessment calendar:* The syllabus should also include information on assessment dates, retakes and (if applicable) coursework submission. It happens surprisingly (and depressingly) often that students are prepared for a public examination, which either was never scheduled as assumed, or has since been withdrawn. Check the future availability of examinations before teaching starts. Even if the detailed timetable is not finalised, the examinations board should publish examinations availability at least a year in advance. In the case of modular (also known as unitised) qualifications, you should bear in mind that some students will want to take re-sits.
- *Qualification level:* In Europe, Australia and New Zealand qualifications are assigned to a level within a qualifications framework, based on the complexity and challenge of skills and knowledge required. Most thinking skills qualifications are at Level 3 of the European Qualifications Framework. Level 3 is aimed at students aged 16-plus and preparing for university entrance, or working independently, or working in a supervisory role. Learning at this level involves obtaining detailed knowledge and skills.
- *Results and grading:* Results for diagnostic tests are usually issued either as a percentage or mark out of the maximum available mark. The marks may be converted into straight Pass/Fail results, often with the Pass mark being predetermined. Results for standalone qualifications may be issued on a straightforward Pass/Fail basis. Additionally Pass results may be graded, with Pass grades being, typically, A* to E, or less commonly Pass, Merit and Distinction. The grading process broadly involves assigning some form of ranking to each candidate's performance, and then converting marks into grades.
- *Guided learning hours:* The time the school or college needs to commit to the course is indicated in the syllabus by the guided learning hours. It includes time students spend in class and in

supervised study, but strictly speaking not homework. The figure for guided learning hours provides a rough indication of whether the qualification can be taught in the available timetable slot, but is not an absolute. Self-motivated, high-achieving students might be able to complete the course with reduced class contact time, and plenty of homework exercises. However, you should not expect students to achieve a thinking skills qualification in significantly less time than would be allocated for a comparable qualification in a different subject.

Finding the right test or qualification

1. Spend time reading suitable syllabuses, question papers and mark schemes. Compare the demands of the different assessments. The style of question papers for any examination evolves over time, so ensure you have some recent past papers.
2. If the board offers briefing events for teachers new to the syllabus, then try to attend one.
3. Try answering a recent past paper from each of the available syllabuses for yourself. Better still, ask colleagues to carry out the same exercise. Mark one another's answers using the mark scheme.
4. If you could not answer the question paper adequately, consider whether you will be able to teach the syllabus effectively. The same applies if you cannot follow why the mark scheme rewards one answer rather than another.
5. Check the future timetable of examinations and whether they will fit the proposed teaching pattern. Make sure that the board does not plan to update or withdraw the qualification in the near future: they will not provide a solution if you have taught a syllabus they no longer offer.
6. Find out what support is available. It is easier to teach with confidence when plenty of teaching and practice material can be obtained. If there is a choice of syllabuses, this can be the clincher. Such support may include teacher guides, e-communities, network meetings, training sessions delivered by senior examiners and syllabus-specific textbooks.
7. Try to contact one or two schools or colleges in your area that already offer the qualification. A quick phone call can be very productive for honest advice and, if you are lucky, the chance to exchange resources. Some exam boards will let you have the names of one or two institutions if you ask.

Preparing students for examinations that make particular intellectual demands

Assessment of thinking skills, especially critical thinking, may appear to offer assessment not of achievement, but of aptitude and potential for achievement, untainted by coaching or by the influence of the candidate's social and other baggage. Some institutions work on the basis that students do not need a major programme of exam preparation and practice for thinking skills assessments. With depressing inevitability, the outcome is usually that students fail to achieve as well as they could have. The evidence is that training and practice do have an impact on candidates' performance in thinking skills tests. It is common for re-sit candidates to improve their performance.

Because thinking skills syllabuses do not necessarily incorporate an obvious body of subject content, schools and colleges often fail to appreciate that it takes time to acquire thinking skills. Candidates should not be expected to prepare for a thinking skills examination in less time than for other subjects at the equivalent level.

Bearing assessment in mind during teaching

You will wish to maintain a balance between making the course interesting and enabling students to achieve good examination results. Students need different forms of preparation for the examination:

- the right subject knowledge and skills;
- general test technique;
- familiarity with what to expect in the test they will be taking.

Towards the start of the course, give out a handout that summarises the syllabus content, and gives straightforward information about the examinations they will be taking i.e. length of examination, question types, the proportion that each paper contributes to the final result, and when the exams should be taken.

Use available opportunities to familiarise students with tasks that employ the various command words they will meet in the examination; for example:

- identify – state;
- describe – give a detailed account of;
- explain – make clear in detail;
- analyse – break down reasoning into constituent parts, giving labels to each part;
- evaluate – assess the strengths and weaknesses of reasoning.

There is no substitute for plenty of practice using questions from past question papers, and this can be interspersed amongst group work and class discussions. Not all exam practice needs to be based around complete past papers: introduce short timed written exercises based on part-questions from previous papers. Start this fairly early in the course to help students learn to manage their time in the exam.

Students can mark one another's answers using the relevant sections of the board-issued mark schemes. Not only will this help them appreciate that examiners look for specific points, rather than general ramblings on a topic, but it will also relieve your own marking burden. Getting students to mark their own or another student's response needs to be handled with care, since mark schemes are designed so that examiners know how many marks to allocate; they are not specimens of correct answers.

Be clear as to what extent marks depend on correct use of subject terminology, and semi-technical language such as the labels for flaws and fallacies, or whether marks could be gained for a correct explanation without use of the exact term.

Guidance on successful examination technique

- *Allow reading and thinking time in the exam:* Time spent thinking in an exam testing thinking and reasoning skills is not time wasted. Teach students how to plan their work, and reinforce that they must spend time thinking in the exam. The marks at the end of each question are a good indication of how much time should be spent on it. For example, if the examination time is an hour and the maximum available mark is 30, then each mark equates to less than two minutes' work, because time is needed for reading and thinking.

- *Don't waste time on questions you can't answer:* With multiple choice questions candidates should pick the answer that seems right, then move on. (Check whether or not wrong answers are penalised in multiple choice papers.) For questions requiring written responses, they should write down what comes to mind, then move on to the next question. If there is time at the end, they can revisit questions they are unsure about.

- *Succinct answers succeed:* Compulsory education means years of being encouraged to produce discursive essays and pieces of 'extended writing'. Exam-technique guidance often includes advice that if candidates are not sure of the answer, they should write what they can before moving on. For most students, it is counter-intuitive to be told that they need to be precise, even minimal, in their responses in the critical thinking exam, and that extraneous verbiage may turn a correct response into an incorrect one. However, despite being counter-intuitive, it is the case in thinking and reasoning examinations. Furthermore, carefully thought-through, well-planned short answers tend to demonstrate a much higher level of thinking and reasoning skills than long rambling answers in which the candidate has dived in pen first, brain lagging lamentably behind.

- *Positive marking:* This does not mean that the examiner likes to be generous with marks. It means that marks are awarded for responses that hit the content of the mark scheme. Other than some multiple choice assessments, marks are not deducted for wrong answers.

- *Holistic marking:* Holistic marking involves looking at a candidate's whole response and judging the quality against objective criteria. It is not woolly, imprecise or especially subjective. This form of marking is generally used when skills are synthesised and applied at a high level, rather than demonstrated in isolation.

- *Use of English (spelling, punctuation and grammar):* The importance placed on grammar and spelling in examinations is a topic where passions can run high amongst teachers and examiners. In thinking skills they are every bit as important as in any other examination. Poor grammar and spelling impede the reader's understanding, and the thinking skills examiner is looking for clarity and accuracy in answers. It is common practice for marks to be awarded for the answer so long as grammatical and spelling errors do not hinder understanding, but you should check the guidance in the syllabus you are teaching. Marks may be awarded specifically for candidates' use of English, or may be subsumed within the marks for the questions. As a rule, the proportion of marks linked to use of English is low, but candidates still fail to gain them by mis-spellings such as 'arguement' and 'credability'. Whilst examiners are professionals, incorrect spelling of words that are intrinsic to the subject tends to annoy them. In practice, the marks candidates achieve for quality of written communication often correlate closely with marks awarded for the rest of the paper.

- *Answer the question:* Every piece of exam-technique advice ever written probably included this instruction. But it still bears repeating. Ad nauseam. Not answering the question is probably the most common reason for apparently able candidates not scoring highly. Candidates find a rich variety of ways to get this wrong. Some – usually the poorly prepared – adopt a scattergun approach and write what comes to mind on the subject that the question seems to be about. 'State one reason which would counter the argument that dogs make ideal pets' triggers random information about dogs. One acceptable answer would be 'Dogs need taking for regular walks, and many people do not have time for this.'

Sometimes candidates trot out the essay they submitted for a different subject, or they reproduce an argument they have written in class, even though it is irrelevant. On other occasions they answer the question they wished they had been asked. For example, the question might read, 'How effectively has the author responded to counter-argument?' Candidates may have practised answering the question 'How effectively has the author supported his main conclusion?', and proceed to do so, even though this question had not been asked. It is very rare for the tactics described here to attract many marks.

Exam tips for students
The exam tips in the text box can be given to students.

Exam tips
Practise the skills as much as possible.
Read the passage carefully.
Answer the question.
Check your answers.
Thinking time is essential.
Independent thought will be rewarded if it is
    supported with sound reasoning.
Succinct answers succeed.
Evidence from the passage may support your
    answer.

9

Managing the Assessment Process

Road Map for Dealing with Examination Boards

What should you expect from an examination board?

The services provided by an exam board falls into two categories: essential information enabling teachers to teach qualifications, and 'added value' in the form of support that schools can choose whether or not to buy into. As a minimum, an exam board should provide:

- regulations for centres, examination regulations; e.g. on invigilation, re-sits, special consideration applications;
- a syllabus document that includes information on the content to be tested, the assessment model, and how results are calculated and graded;
- sample question papers and mark schemes;
- past question papers and mark schemes;
- senior examiners' reports on each examination;
- the examination timetable;
- information on how re-marks, results enquiries and appeals against results can be initiated;
- information on how centres can complain;
- teacher support, such as training events (which may be charged) led by senior examiners who provide guidance on preparing students and feedback on recent examinations.

What if the question paper isn't a fair test of the syllabus?

Reassure students (and if necessary their parents).

Comments, concerns and complaints should be taken into account as part of normal examination procedures, but they need to be received promptly so they can be acted on when examiners are trained and when the awarding committee decides where the grade boundaries should be set. A measured explanation of concerns relating to specific questions will be taken seriously, but don't expect more than a standard response initially – the board is probably dealing with thousands of results within tight deadlines. However, if there was a mistake in the question paper, then marking guidance will be amended to ensure scripts are marked fairly. If necessary, problematic questions may be completely discounted.

What if students' results do not match expectations?

When a school enters students for a thinking skills examination subject for the first time, students' results do not necessarily turn out as expected: some may be better than projected, others worse. As with any other examination subject that has not been taught before, such problems are partly down to lack of experience in the subject, and often to failure to appreciate the requirements of the examination in terms of precision and accuracy.

It is also important to bear in mind that achievement in critical thinking does not necessarily mirror students' performance in their other subjects. The awarding bodies' results for England and Wales in GCE A Level Critical Thinking in both 2008 and 2009 showed lower percentages of passes and A grades than in any other subject. It is unclear whether this also results from endemic lack of subject experience, or is because standards have been set comparatively higher than in other subjects. There is, however, evidence of high correlation between grades achieved in critical thinking and in numerate subjects, particularly physics and economics, and likewise evidence of poorer correlation with essay-based subjects such as English literature.[12]

In England and Wales A Level and GCSE examinations are highly regulated through the Office of the Qualifications and Examinations Regulator (Ofqual). In practice, this means that examiners are expected to have experience of teaching the subject they mark and must participate in training before they can mark a particular paper. Their work is monitored by more senior examiners, who re-mark a proportion of each examiner's work. In addition, statistical data can be used to identify examiners whose marking is erratic.

Despite this careful quality assurance, the number of A Level and re-marked GCSE scripts has increased steadily in the last ten years. This may be due to modularisation of qualifications, which has led to candidates taking more examinations than ever before. It may also be due to consumers – of any product, including public examinations – being more willing to complain. Nonetheless, the proportion of re-marks that lead to changed results is very small: fewer than one in a thousand GCE A Level papers re-marked in the summer of 2009 resulted in grade changes (see www.ofqual. gov.uk).

So examiners do not always get the marking (or the clerical processes) right, but there are other reasons why students may fail to achieve the grades expected, including unsuitable preparation and unrealistic expectations. These two factors often lead to disappointing results, especially when the school is new to the subject. In this situation, the strategy needs to consist of:

- reviewing results;
- deciding whether to request re-marks or return of scripts;
- establishing whether results accurately reflect students' performance;
- learning from re-marks or the return of scripts;
- reviewing the course, resources and teaching;
- putting in place mechanisms for improvement.

These are considered in detail below.

Reviewing results and deciding whether to request re-marks or return of scripts

First reactions when students receive their results can be highly charged, especially if the results are lower than expected. You need to work quickly to decide whether there is a case for asking the examination board to review results.

It is important that a realistic appraisal is made of possible causes of poor results, not least because students' hopes may be raised unjustifiably if they are told that the school intends to raise concerns with the exam board. The guidance below will help you decide whether examination results need investigation at the board. Then take time to allow the dust to settle before carrying out a course review and making changes designed to enable the next cohort to achieve better results.

Establishing whether results accurately reflect students' performance

If results for the qualification are reported as marks or grades, check whether the rank order is more or less as expected for that subject. If not, then it may indicate that the examiner's marking was erratic. When a breakdown of marks is provided for different components, check whether results for any one component are significantly out of line with the others.

Do not attach too much significance to the relationship (or lack of it) between actual results and the forecasts you submitted to the board. Exam boards use teacher forecasts for a variety of purposes and, contrary to popular belief, they are not normally used for a direct check on individual results. The forecasts enable measures of the ability of the whole cohort to be calculated. If an individual script has been lost, or the student missed the examination due to illness, than a result can still be issued based on the forecast. Finally, teacher forecasts, taken with other information, provide a means of identifying examiners whose marking needs checking.

Check whether the grades correlate *roughly* with students' results in other subjects. But be careful: performance in assessments of critical thinking does not necessarily correlate directly with performance in other subjects. Anecdotal and other evidence suggests a high correlation between numerate subjects, such as physics or economics, and critical thinking. Lower correlations have been reported between subjects such as English literature and critical thinking.

If there was a different cohort entered for a previous examination in this subject at this level, then check whether there is a marked shift in the range of results. Consider whether there have been changes in the way the course was taught. Again, bear in mind that the range of ability can be very different across small groups of students.

UK examination boards issue national statistics for most qualifications and it can be interesting to review your students' results against national figures. Remember that the results achieved by a small group of students are unlikely to follow quite the same pattern as that of the cohort nationally.

The conclusion may indeed be that the results do not accurately reflect students' abilities. If so, then the issue is whether results are disappointing because they were not properly prepared for the test, or because there has been erratic marking – or possibly both.

Clerical checks, re-marks and return of scripts from the exam board

UK examination boards issue guidance on the procedures that centres must follow to request either a clerical check, re-mark or the return of scripts, all known in officialese as enquiries about results.

Do not imagine you can short-circuit the process by threats or appeals to the better nature of the board's officers: they have heard sob stories before and their job is to make sure candidates are all treated fairly and in line with the rules. Increasingly, boards operate common procedures and use common paperwork. There is no flexibility about the procedure, which in the case of UK exam boards is regulated by the government agency, Ofqual.

Make sure you:

- work with your centre's examinations officer or head teacher to instigate the results enquiry;
- refer to the board's regulations to find out the procedure and the paperwork;
- use the correct form and provide all the information asked for (missing or wrong information will delay the process);

- check whether the outcome of any re-mark could lead to results going down as well as up, and warn the student;
- ensure the student understands the implications of the results enquiry, and get their agreement (or their parents') in writing;
- work fast: you need to meet tight deadlines, and the sooner the board receives the enquiry, the sooner it will be dealt with (if the student's university place depends on the outcome, and there is a priority results service, then seriously consider using it);
- remember that there is usually a charge for any enquiry about results, although this may be refunded if the result is changed.

There are three different forms of enquiries about results:

1. *A clerical check:* This simply checks that all questions were marked and the marks have been added up correctly.
2. *Re-marks:* These are carried out by a different examiner to the original marker, normally one who is more senior, and whose previous marking has been judged reliable. An effective strategy may be to identify just one or two scripts for re-marking, where you have serious concerns. If the re-marking confirms the original marking was seriously in error, then the board should automatically re-mark other scripts in the same batch. There is no harm in asking if this will happen.

   If the original result is confirmed by the re-mark, and you still believe it was wrong, then you can appeal. It is important to bear in mind that you cannot appeal because you disagree with the examiners' marking, or because you think the mark scheme content is wrong. An appeal can be made only on the basis that the board has failed to apply procedures correctly. In a first-stage appeal, the script, and your reasons for the appeal, will be reviewed by someone within the board who has had no previous involvement with the re-marking of that script. There may a further stage of appeal within the board's own processes. This is far more formal, and will involve you presenting your case to a panel, who also hear the board's case before reaching their decision. The panel cannot change the result, but they can, and often do, require the board to re-mark the script again using a clean copy. There is a final stage of appeal to the Examinations Appeals Board.

   Although there are tight deadlines for the different stages of appeal, the whole process can be long drawn out. Unfortunately, by the time the procedure is completed, students have often moved onto the next stage of their studies.

The rules for re-marks may be subject to amendment from one year to the next. You should not even consider asking for re-marks without checking the current rules, which can be downloaded from boards' websites.

3. *Return of scripts:* This is intended to help teachers understand how the examination was assessed and help their students improve their performance. You can request either photocopies of scripts or the actual scripts. Once the actual script is returned, you cannot ask for it to be re-marked, should you conclude that the original marking was inaccurate. If you get back a photocopy, then it might still be possible to ask for a re-mark. Exam boards normally publish their turnaround times for returning scripts, which should happen quite fast.

- Requesting return of two or three actual scripts should be done only if there is absolutely no chance of the student wanting a re-mark. Boards will not accept a request for a result to be reviewed once a script has been returned, no matter how glaring the examiner errors uncovered.
- Pick scripts awarded grades that seem particularly out of sync with predictions.
- Requesting return of photocopies of the script is likely to take longer than requesting the actual scripts.
- Check that marks have been added up correctly and check the marking against the published mark scheme. Review returned scripts against the published mark scheme and examiners' report. Bear in mind that examiners would have received detailed training in the use of the mark scheme and that mark schemes are not exhaustive. However, a re-mark should still be possible if you find marking errors in a returned script photocopy.

Boards will not normally enter into correspondence on the details of marking, but if you have a genuine concern, put it in a letter, ensuring this is short and to the point.

Course review

The fact that grades predicted were over-optimistic does not automatically mean that the cause lies primarily with the subject teacher. When the course is reviewed, the questions below should be considered.

Resourcing

- Has the institution fully supported the subject? If not, then it is likely that this had an impact on the teacher's commitment and on resources.
- Was the groundwork done before teaching started? Was the teacher allowed time to prepare materials and released to attend training events offered by the exam board? Could other centres teaching the same syllabus have been approached to share expertise?
- Did the time allocation and the class size promote development of critical thinking? Schools sometimes assume incorrectly that critical thinking can be taught to examination standard in less time than other subjects. This can work with a small group of eager high-achievers who have opted to take critical thinking. It is less likely to be a successful strategy if critical thinking is compulsory. Critical thinking content can be covered relatively quickly, but activities that promote thinking skills, such as inquiry and discussion, require time.
- Was the subject adequately resourced? In particular, do textbooks provide content and tasks relevant in preparation for the exam?

Teaching

- Was the teacher a willing volunteer with enthusiasm for critical thinking or an unfortunate who was railroaded into it? Either way, the teacher may not have been fully committed or may have felt that thinking skills detracted from teaching their main subject. Staff who have not bought into thinking skills may inadvertently give out negative messages. They may consider they are already teaching critical thinking, or that academic high-flyers can already think critically.
- Does the teacher possess the necessary expertise? There is no evidence that a background in either arts, humanities or sciences produces a more successful teacher of CT. What is *not* recommended is that a discrete thinking skills course is added to a teacher's timetable because they happen to be 'short on their hours'. After all, schools would not ask an English teacher to teach advanced physics because they had space on the timetable. Nonetheless, teachers may not be confident of their own critical thinking skills. Very often the teacher's own education did not support thinking skills development. Specific training is not included in teacher training courses. Teachers have not therefore absorbed a model for teaching thinking skills.

- Was the syllabus the best choice? Assuming there was a choice of suitable qualifications, was the one selected the most suitable for the cohort? GCE A Levels, for example, are all theoretically of comparable standard, but different syllabuses make different demands in terms of content and assessment style. Together with the textbook and resource materials, the teaching might have led to knowledge acquisition rather than development of critical thinking. Students bring different knowledge and aptitudes to the subject, and the style of examination might not have enabled them to play to their strengths.

Students

- Did the students opt in or were discrete thinking skills classes compulsory? Irrespective of their other abilities, most students are highly skilled subversives when they don't want to participate.
- Did students sit examinations too early in the course? Thinking skills are interdependent and develop over time. Students need maturity to tackle thinking skills assessments successfully.
- Have students had enough practice with past examination papers? If so, were they given focused feedback based on the board's examiner reports and mark schemes?

The repair kit

There is no substitute for finding out what examiners are looking for when they mark scripts. If the exam board provides feedback meetings after the exam session, then you should book a place. An even better way to learn more about assessment of the subject is to become an examiner yourself.

Research indicates that the most successful thinking skills programmes combine discrete skills lessons and embedding the skills in all curriculum areas. Both a whole-institution approach, and the type of resources described above, help enormously. However, enthusiastic individual teachers have achieved impressive results with their students in relatively unpromising situations.

Teachers whose students achieve well in thinking skills assessments have certain key traits. First, they are willing to engage with students, reflect on their own practice and alter their approach. Above all, the best results are achieved when *the teacher can think*. That means being able to reason, rather than having been trained in formal or informal logic. It also means questioning evidence, challenging accepted 'facts', respecting unorthodox opinions and welcoming students' contributions – bizarre or otherwise.

Endnotes

1 The online material contains details of textbooks which deal with reasoning skills.

2 See www.oxfam.org.uk/resources/policy/conflict_disasters/dangers-of-militarized-aid-afghanistan.html. Another direction the discussion here could take is how likely it really is that a charity report like this one (as opposed to advertising campaign) would exaggerate a situation in order to encourage people to make donations. Here, however, the teacher has allowed that comment to pass as part of the student's thinking process, and picked up on the (more) important issue that an assessment of credibility can tell us only about the quality of the evidence, not about the conclusions and opinions based on or contained in that evidence.

3 Ian Gilbert, *The Little Book of Thunks: 260 Questions to Make Your Brain Go Ouch!* Crown House Publishing Ltd, Carmarthen, 2007, p. 43.

4 Ibid., p. 40.

5 There are a number of useful websites that explore Bloom's Taxonomy, including: http://projects.coe.uga.edu/epltt/index.php?title=Bloom%27s_Taxonomy.

6 Cf. Bloom's Taxonomy.

7 Most critical thinking textbooks have some guidance on showing argument structure. There are different ways of doing this; so long as it remains a tool used for a purpose and not an isolated formula performed for its own sake, any can be useful.

8 A multiplicity of thinking skills frameworks and classification systems has been developed. In one project, 35 different classifications, ranging from Bloom's (1956) to Marzano's (2001), were categorised and reviewed (LSDA report on taxonomies).

9 Remarks of the President to the United States Hispanic Chamber of Commerce – The White House Office of the Press Secretary, 10 March 2009, http://www.whitehouse.gov/the-press-office/remarks-president-united-states-hispanic-chamber-commerce.

10 For non-UK readers, achieving a 'qualification' means you have successfully completed a course or assessment and demonstrated a particular level of skill or knowledge in a subject. This is recognised by the issue of an award, certificate, diploma or degree, from a relevant formal body, which indicates that the individual has achieved learning outcomes, competencies or fitness for employment or further study. Some qualifications confirm a licence to act in a specific profession.

11 Dona Warren's *Standardized Critical Thinking Assessment Tools 1: College-Level Critical Thinking Exams* is a very thorough list of assessments available in the USA. See www.uwsp.edu/special/wact/WACTConference2007/WarrenCTExams.pdf.

12 Beth Black quoted in 'Do candidates who have taken Critical Thinking AS level perform better in their A levels in other subjects?', article in *Achieve*, Summer 2008, published by Cambridge Assessment.

References

Adey, P. S., Shayer, M. and Yates, C. (1995), *Thinking Science: The Curriculum Materials of the CASE Project*, London: Thomas Nelson and Sons.

Bailin, S., Case, R., Coombs, J. R. and Daniels, L. B. (1999), 'Common Misconceptions of Critical Thinking', *Journal of Curriculum Studies* 31 (3), pp. 269–83; www.tanf.co.uk;JNLS/cus.htm.

Bailin, S., Case, R., Coombs, J. R. and Daniels, L. B. (1993), 'A Conception of Critical Thinking for Curriculum, Instruction and Assessment', Paper commissioned by the Examinations Branch, BC Ministry of Education and Ministry Responsible for Multiculturalism and Human Rights in conjunction with the Curriculum Development Branch and the Research and Evaluation Branch. Victoria, BC: Ministry of Education.

Barack Obama (2009), Remarks of the President to the United States Hispanic Chamber of Commerce – The White House Office of the Press Secretary, 10 March 2009, www.whitehouse.gov/the-press-office/remarks-president-united-states-hispanic-chamber-commerce.

BBC (2007), 'Increase in top grades at A-level', Thursday 16 August 2007; http://news.bbc.co.uk/1/hi/education/6949084.stm.

Birkhead, Tim (2009), 'We've bred a generation unable to think', *Times Educational Supplement*, 7 February; www.tes.co.uk/article.aspx?storycode=6008340.

Black, B. (2008), 'Critical Thinking – A Definition and Taxonomy, for Cambridge Assessment', Paper presented at 34th International Association of Educational Assessment Annual Conference, Cambridge, *Research Matters* 6 (June), pp. 30–35.

Blagg, N., Ballinger, M. and Gardner, R. (2003), *Somerset Thinking Skills Handbook*, *Revised Edition*, published by Nigel Blagg Associates in association with Somerset County Council.

Butchart, S., Forster, D., Gold, I., Bigelow, J. Korb, K. Oppy, G. and Serrenti, A. (2009), 'Improving Critical Thinking using Web-based Argument Mapping Exercises with Automated Feedback',

Australasian Journal of Educational Technology 25 (2), pp. 268–91.

Center for Critical Thinking (for various materials published see www. criticalthinking.org).

De Bono, Edward (1967), *The Use of Lateral Thinking* (London: Jonathan Cape, 1967); www.edwdebono.com.

Dewey, John (1909), *Moral Principles in Education*, first published by The Riverside Press, Cambridge, Massachusetts, p. 9.

DfES (2004), Key Stage 3 National Strategy Pedagogy and Practice Unit 16: 'Leading in Learning', DfES 0439-2004 (www.nationalstrategies. standards.dcsf.gov.uk).

Ennis, Robert (1996), *An Annotated List of Critical Thinking Tests Prepared by Robert H. Ennis*, University of Illinois, revised July 2006 (at the time of writing this needed updating, but it is nonetheless a useful exposition of different types of thinking skills assessments); http://faculty.ed.uiuc.edu/rhennis/testlistrevised606. htm.

European Commission Directorate-General for Education and Culture (2004), *Key Competences for Lifelong Learning – A European Reference Framework*, European Commission, November.

Facione, Peter A. (1990), *Critical Thinking: A Statement of Expert Consensus for Purposes of Educational Assessment and Instruction* (The Delphi Report), Millbrae, California: The California Academic Press.

Fisher, Alec and Scriven, Michael (1997), *Critical Thinking: Its Definition and Assessment*, University of East Anglia, Centre for Research in Critical Thinking, November.

Government of Quebec (2001), *Programme de formation de l'école québécoise – Éducation préscolaire, Enseignement primaire, version approuvée* [Aménagement Linguistique Policy in the Education Sector in Ontario], Quebec: Ministry of Education / Ministère de l'Éducation Gouvernement du Québec, ISBN 2-550-37958-6 [www.gouv.qc.ca], p. 20.

Halpern, Diane F. (1997), *Critical Thinking across the Curriculum: A Brief Edition of Thought and Knowledge*, Mahwah, NJ: Lawrence Erlbaum Associates.

Halpin, Tony (Education Editor) (2005), 'Grammar sets record in fight to top tables', *The Times*, 19 August; www.timesonline.co.uk/tol/ life_and_style/education/article556828.ece.

Halpin, Tony and Blair, Alexandra (2006), 'A critical extra edge for leading grammar', *The Times*, 19 January; www.timesonline.co.uk/tol/ life_and_style/education/school_league_tables/article792863.ece.

Leat, David (ed.) (and Simon Chandler) (1998), *Thinking Through Geography*, Chris Kington Publishing.

Lipman, M., Sharp, A. M. and Oscanyan, F. S. (2003), *Philosophy in the Classroom*, 2nd edn, Philadelphia: Temple University Press.

McGuinness, C. (1999), *From Thinking Skills to Thinking Classrooms: A Review and Evaluation of Approaches for Developing Pupils' Thinking*, Research Report No. 115, Nottingham: DfEE Publications.

McPeck, J. E. (1981), *Critical Thinking and Education*, Oxford, UK: Martin Robertson.

Ofqual (2009), *The Reliability Programme*, Technical Seminar Report – 7 October 2009, published December; www.ofqual.gov.uk/files/Reliability_Programme_Technical_Seminar_Report.pdf.

Sternberg, Robert J. (1986), *Critical Thinking: Its Nature, Measurement, and Improvement*, Washington, DC: National Institute of Education; www.eric.ed.gov, see ED272882.

Tan, Charlene (2006), 'Creating Thinking Schools through "Knowledge and Inquiry": The Curriculum Challenges for Singapore', *Curriculum Journal* 17 (1), (March), pp. 89–105.

Van Gelder, T., Bissett, M. and and Cumming, G. (2004), 'Cultivating Expertise in Informal Reasoning', *Canadian Journal of Experimental Psychology* 58 (2), pp. 142–52; www.philosophy.unimelb.edu.au/reason/papers/CJEP_van_Gelder.pdf.

Wilson, Valerie (2000), *Can Thinking Skills be Taught?* Report for the Scottish Executive Education Department and the Scottish Council for Research in Education (SCRE) Forum on Teaching Thinking Skills, 15 May, Spotlights series, No. 79, p. 7; www.scre.ac.uk/spotlight/index.html.

Index

(Entries in bold, followed by an asterisk, denote material in the online section)